NEW YORK
THEN AND NOW

83 MANHATTAN SITES PHOTOGRAPHED
IN THE PAST AND IN THE PRESENT

CAPTIONS BY EDWARD B. WATSON

CONTEMPORARY PHOTOGRAPHS BY EDMUND V. GILLON, JR.

DOVER PUBLICATIONS, INC., NEW YORK

Published in Canada by General Publishing Company, Ltd., 30 Lesmill Road, Don Mills, Toronto, Ontario.
Published in the United Kingdom by Constable and Company, Ltd., 10 Orange Street, London WC 2.

New York Then and Now is a new work, first published by Dover Publications, Inc., in 1976.

International Standard Book Number: 0-486-23361-8
Library of Congress Catalog Card Number: 76-3240

Manufactured in the United States of America
Dover Publications, Inc.
180 Varick Street
New York, N.Y. 10014

PUBLISHER'S NOTE

This book contrasts photographic views of New York taken between 1864 and 1938 with views of the same sites as they appeared in 1974-75. Forty-eight of the early photographs are taken from the extensive and diverse Seidman historical archive; 38 have been supplied from Mr. Watson's collection. There was considerable choice in selecting this material; since the first daguerreotype was taken of New York in 1839, it has been one of the most extensively photographed cities. The plates have been chosen to represent the major thoroughfares and districts of Manhattan. No attempt has been made to dramatize the degree and nature of change in the city or to make the book conform to any particular opinion about the implications of change.

In contrast to the more artistic (and famous) photographs of the city taken at the turn of the century by such photographers as Edward Steichen and Alfred Stieglitz, most of the pictures in this volume were taken by anonymous photographers for didactic purposes. In matching them, Mr. Gillon has adhered to a similar straightforward approach: his lighting is even and his prints are developed to maximize detail; he has not strived for artistic "effect." He has made every effort to match the original vantage points as closely as possible but, in a few instances, physical alterations at a site have necessitated some shift of angle. In some scenes, such as the pair of views of Madison Avenue, looking south from East 31st Street (pp. 92, 93), distances and proportions do not appear to correspond. This phenomenon is caused not by a change of vantage point, but by differences between the two photographers' equipment.

It is curious that, although countless photographs of the city have been taken, there has never been any project to record, in a systematic and thorough manner, the appearance of the city at a given time. Even though Mr. Gillon has taken only 83 photographs, this book is a step in that direction. As a further aid, the date and time (always during daylight hours) at which each photograph was taken is recorded at the end of each caption for the modern photographs. (In many of the older photographs, this information can be established only on the basis of internal evidence.)

In keeping with the straightforward nature of the photographs, Mr. Watson has confined himself to fact in writing the captions. With little editorial comment, he notes trends and changes in architecture, transportation and other characteristics of the city. For the most part, the reader is left to form his own opinions about the development and changing nature of New York.

The photographs reveal many obvious changes to the browser—the passing of the horse and the subsequent proliferation of traffic, the development of high-rise buildings, and the evolution of women's fashions. Many less obvious changes are revealed only through study. One can observe shifts in ethnic and racial populations and changes in patterns of land use and development. During the last century, for example, it was inconceivable that a landowner would not build on a parcel in a developed section of the city, yet today parking lots and "fallow" properties are seen everywhere. It also becomes apparent that, while some aspects of the city have changed radically, exceeding the wildest imaginings of nineteenth-century writers, other aspects remain virtually the same. There is little to differentiate today's sidewalk food vendor from his counterpart of 1900.

Change is New York's identifying trait. Compared with other cities, its buildings have a very short life span. Stanford White's Presbyterian Church, an outstanding piece of architecture, stood for only 13 years before it was razed. What will the city look like 100 years from now? One would like to think that another edition of this book will be published then, recording, from the same vantage points, the changes brought about by subsequent waves of demolition and construction.

NEW YORK
THEN AND NOW

83 MANHATTAN SITES PHOTOGRAPHED
IN THE PAST AND IN THE PRESENT

Broadway, North from State Street, Looking toward Bowling Green (1914)

Here is the beginning of Broadway, New York's greatest street. The edge of the Customs House (right) shows Daniel Chester French's allegorical group *Africa*, one of the *Four Continents* group. The Washington Building is located on the left-hand corner; the Bowling Green Building is just beyond. Behind the only double-deck streetcar ever to run in New York City is the great canyon of lower Broadway. The steel construction with finished courses of white brick, visible at left center, is the Adams Express Building. Farther along on the west side of Broadway stands the tower of the Singer Building. In the distance is the recently completed Woolworth Building, then the world's tallest structure.

Broadway, North from State Street, Looking toward Bowling Green (1974)

In late 1974, Bowling Green, New York's first public park, was being reconstructed to conform with the plan of 1786. The former Customs House, with the sculptured group *Africa*, stands unchanged and the Bowling Green Building remains at the extreme left. Beyond Bowling Green, on the east side of Broadway, is the huge No. 26 Broadway Building, originally built for the Standard Oil Co. in 1924. It took the place of the three office buildings on the site. Looking up

Broadway, the former Adams Express Building (now American Express), with a dark cornice, still remains. The Singer Tower is gone, but in its place is the new United States Steel Building, the top of its black structure visible to the right of the American Express Building. In the center, the Woolworth Tower continues to dominate lower Broadway. (9/30/74; 3:15.)

Trinity Churchyard, Looking North to Broadway and Pine Street (1890)

This view of part of the north section of the Trinity Church graveyard shows a number of aged gravestones, some dating from the last half of the seventeenth century. Many well-known New Yorkers were buried here, among them Alexander Hamilton and Robert Fulton. Even though this graveyard is located in the midst of the busy downtown financial district, it offers a sense of repose and quiet. All the various office buildings shown here have been demolished during the past fifty years. The large structure in the center is the headquarters of the Equitable Life Assurance Society, occupying a full acre of ground from Broadway to Nassau Street and from Pine to Cedar Streets. The building was destroyed by fire on January 9, 1912. The building on the left is the six-story Trinity Building, designed in 1852 by the famous architect Richard Upjohn, who designed the present Trinity Church.

Trinity Churchyard, Looking North to Broadway and Pine Street (1974)

There has been very little change in the churchyard. Some low hedges and railings have been added as protection. The large brownstone monument with the small steeple (hidden by a tree in the 1890 photo) is the Martyrs' Memorial, erected in 1858 in memory of the soldiers of the American Revolution who died in prison during the British occupation of New York (1776-83). The building on the right, undergoing first-floor renovation, is the 22-story American Surety Co., built in 1894 and greatly enlarged in 1920. The building in the center is the 38-story Equitable Life Building, built in 1913-15 on the site of the firm's older building. It was the world's largest office building from 1915 until 1931. On the left is the 21-story second Trinity Building, erected in 1904 on the site of the original Trinity Building. (12/3/74; 12:40.)

Park Row, Looking Southwest toward Broadway (1892)

The beginning of Park Row at Broadway, with suitable loop and storage tracks, was a busy terminal for horsecar lines. The six-story granite building on the right, at the northwest corner of Broadway and Vesey Street, is the Astor House, the leading downtown hotel. Originally called the Park Hotel and designed by Isaiah Rogers, it was built in 1832-36 on the site of the residence of John Jacob Astor, who also owned the hotel. It was favored by celebrities until the imposing Fifth Avenue Hotel was opened in 1858 at Fifth Avenue and 23rd Street. The Astor House's rotunda lunchroom was the most popular eating place in downtown New York. St. Paul's Chapel (Thomas MacBean, architect) is the oldest church and public building in New York. It was erected on Broadway, between Vesey and Fulton Streets, in 1764-66 as a chapel of Trinity Church. The portico was added in 1768. The clock tower with steeple, modeled on James Gibbs's St. Martin's-in-the-Fields, London, was built in 1794. The front of the chapel was designed to face the fine view of the Hudson River. The stone chapel is famous not only for its architecture and antiquity but also for the pew, still preserved, that George Washington occupied while he was in New York. The L-shaped structure beyond the chapel is the Mail and Express Building, designed by Henry J. Hardenbergh and built in 1891.

Park Row, Looking Southwest toward Broadway (1974)

Park Row is used as a turning loop for several important New York City bus lines. In 1914 the south half of the Astor House was demolished to make way for the Astor House Office Building, now the Franklin Society Federal Savings & Loan headquarters (Charles A. Platt, architect). The north half of the Astor House came down in 1927, and York & Sawyer's 43-story Transportation Building, part of which is visible at the right, was built on the site. St. Paul's Chapel, although hemmed in by numerous tall buildings, remains New York's outstanding landmark and an architectural gem. At the left, on the Fulton Street side of St. Paul's, is the American Telephone & Telegraph Building, designed by W. W. Bosworth, which took the place of the Mail and Express Building in 1922. The two huge 110-story World Trade Center towers rise in the background. Recently completed, they were for a short time the tallest buildings in the world, until Chicago's Sears Tower claimed the title in 1973. (12/3/74; 12:35.)

West Side of Broadway, South from Park Place (1880)

It must have been early on a quiet Sunday morning that this photo was taken; there are few pedestrians and the only traffic is a horsecar of the Broadway and Seventh Avenue line, waiting on Park Place to start its uptown run to 59th Street. The five-story Berkshire Life Insurance Building on the corner was built in 1852, the year after the founding of the Broadway Savings Bank, which occupied the first-floor rear section for 55 years. In 1885 two additional stories were added to the building. One block south stands the famous Astor House and directly beyond is the portico of St. Paul's Chapel. The tall structure farther along is the Western Union Telegraph Building, one of the tallest buildings in New York when erected in 1873.

West Side of Broadway, South from Park Place (1974)

The entire west blockfront of Broadway from Park Place to Barclay Street was torn down in 1911 to make way for the world-famous Woolworth Building. When completed in 1913, it was the tallest skyscraper in the world and remained so until 1931. It was designed by Cass Gilbert, already noted for the Customs House at the foot of Broadway. The Woolworth Building is known for its Gothic styling and for its lobby, frequently called the most beautiful in New York. The New York Architectural League awarded its Medal of Honor to Gilbert in 1916 for what it considered one of the country's finest buildings—which it still is. South beyond the Woolworth Building is the Transportation Building (1927) and the six-story Franklin Building (1914), both built on the site of the Astor House. The portico of St. Paul's Chapel, the only building in the 1880 photo still standing, is visible on the block from Vesey to Fulton Streets. On the next block south is the 28-story A.T.&T. Building (1914-22). Towering at Cortlandt Street stands the all-steel United States Steel Building (1972), one of the many built in this style in New York City during recent years. (12/3/74; 1:55.)

Broadway, North from Murray Street (1887)

The edge of City Hall Park is on the right. Left, on the southwest corner of Warren Street, is No. 259 (Devlin & Co.), where Tiffany & Co. was founded in 1837. The white-marble building (Trench & Snook, architects) seen above the trees of City Hall Park was opened in 1848 as the dry-goods store of A. T. Stewart, who moved to a larger store at Broadway and East 9th Street in 1862. In 1885 two stories were added to the building. Omnibuses are seen sharing Broadway with the newer horsecars, which had only been permitted on lower Broadway, after much litigation, since 1885.

Broadway, North from Murray Street (1974)

Broadway remains a busy thoroughfare, and in this section the nature of its business is the same. The marble building has had a further addition—the top-story corner has been filled out. A few of the older buildings can still be seen on Broadway. On the left, the elaborate lower stories of the Home Life Insurance Building (1893-94) remain without alteration. The latest skyscraper, rising on the right, is a new addition to the Federal Building on Foley Square. (9/30/74; 10:20.)

East Side of Broadway, North of East Houston Street (1875)

The Olympic Theatre, at No. 624 Broadway, between Houston and Bleecker Streets, was opened on November 18, 1856, as Laura Keene's Varieties Theatre, but was shortly afterwards renamed Laura Keene's New Theatre. Miss Keene retired as manager of the Olympic in 1863. It was Laura Keene who was appearing in *Our American Cousin* at Ford's Theatre the night President Lincoln was assassinated. The Olympic reopened as Mrs. John Wood's Olympic Theatre after Miss Keene left. Mrs. Wood retired in 1866. George L. Fox appeared at the Olympic in the clown pantomime *Humpty Dumpty*, which opened in March 1868 and ran 483 times (not counting revivals). The house had a varied career and changed hands several times after 1870. The last manager, Frank Mayo, began a season in January 1880 and closed the house on April 17. The building was demolished after a fire in 1881. A variety of businesses appear at Nos. 618-628 Broadway: "New York Museum of Anatomy, Science & Art," a straw-goods concern, the theater (featuring the acrobatic Carlo family), a publishing house sharing a building with a cabinetmaker and a banner painter, and, finally, a carriage builder.

East Side of Broadway, North of East Houston Street (1975)

On the site of the Olympic Theatre at Nos. 622-624 stands a six-story loft building, erected in 1882, with a cast-iron front and iron balconies serving as fire escapes. The larger, six-window-wide section at No. 622 suffered a fire in 1971 which burned out the interior of the four upper floors, but it has been repaired. The one building remaining from the 1875 photo is located on the right, at No. 620. Built in 1858-59, it is one of the oldest cast-iron buildings still standing in New York City. The Mercantile Exchange Building, at No. 628-630, is another cast-iron structure, built in 1882. It was designed by the Philadelphia architect Herman J. Schwarzmann, who created Memorial Hall in the Philadelphia Centennial Exhibition of 1876. The Hall still stands in Fairmount Park as a record of that great celebration. (4/17/75; 2:10.)

Broadway, Looking North from East 10th Street (1911)

Broadway, the longest street in New York City, is also one of the most important, housing many diverse phases of city life such as financial and wholesale sections, shopping and theatrical areas as well as residential, medical and educational centers. Here Broadway approaches Union Square from the south, with what is probably the midday crowd on its wide sidewalks. At this busy time public transportation was the principal means of travel; the photo shows seven streetcars and only one private vehicle (the chauffeur-driven car just behind the streetcar going downtown). The Broadway streetcar line was a convenient route, especially since the subway did not open on this part of

Broadway for another six years. On the right is part of Grace Episcopal Church, erected 1843-46 and designed by James Renwick, Jr., who became the architect of St. Patrick's Cathedral ten years later. The six-story St. Denis Hotel (1852), also designed by Renwick, stands on the left, at the southwest corner of East 11th Street. On the northwest corner of 11th Street is the cast-iron building (1868) occupied by McCreery's store from 1869 until 1902, when it was converted for loft use. In the far center are the trees of Union Square. Farther beyond stands the broad end of the tall Flatiron Building at 23rd Street.

14

Broadway, Looking North from East 10th Street (1975)

It is surprising how many buildings, many over 100 years old, survive without much change on Broadway below 34th Street. Grace Church, one of the many grand old churches of Manhattan, stands on the right, hidden behind the luxuriant trees. A 15-story apartment house was built in 1929 at the northwest corner of East 10th Street (far left) but the adjoining building remains with little change, except for some additions to the fire escape. The former St. Denis Hotel has been renovated into a business building, stripped of its former decorative front. The former McCreery store, its exterior signs removed, stands with an additional story and a fine exterior paint job. In 1973, new owners converted the interior for residential occupancy, giving the 107-year-old

building a new lease on life. In contrast to the unfortunate exterior of the former St. Denis Hotel, this renovation is a splendid example of how interesting architecture can be adapted for varying uses without destroying its esthetic appeal. The 14-story loft building at the southwest corner of East 12th Street (designed by George B. Post and built in 1896) remains unchanged. The entire west block from 12th to 13th Streets, plus the loft building with the beehive-like ornament at the roof corner, remain intact. Emery Roth's 1927 office and store building stands high at the 14th Street corner, while beyond, past Union Square Park, modern office buildings obstruct the view of Broadway farther uptown. (8/8/75; 10:15.)

Broadway, Looking North from West 32nd Street toward Sixth Avenue (1893)

The triangular park where Broadway meets Sixth Avenue at West 33rd Street is named Greeley Square in honor of the journalist, politician and statesman whose statue was unveiled there in 1890. In 1893 Broadway had substituted cable cars for horsecars. Eight years later the electric streetcar took over. The Sixth Avenue elevated line still used small steam locomotives. The Standard Theatre, on the west side of Sixth Avenue between 32nd and 33rd Streets, was formerly the Eagle Theatre. In 1897 it was renamed the Manhattan Theatre. Featuring traveling companies, it remained a legitimate theater until 1908. In 1893 Charles H. Hopper was playing there in *Chimmie Fadden*. Koster & Bial's, a well-known variety house, had recently moved from West 23rd Street to West 34th Street. Its roof sign is at right center. In 1896, the theater featured what were most likely the first commercially projected films in America. Looking up Broadway, at the far right, just beyond the building with the awnings, the old Metropolitan Opera House can be seen at West 39th Street.

Broadway, Looking North from West 32nd Street toward Sixth Avenue (1974)

Three well-known department stores dominate the area today. Gimbels, the 11-story department store on the left, built in 1910, occupies the block from 32nd to 33rd Streets on Sixth Avenue. Korvettes (1967), on the block from 33rd to 34th Streets, rebuilt the old Saks-Herald Square store building, which had been erected in 1902. R. H. Macy's store appears across 34th Street, in the center of the photo. Above 35th Street, Broadway is entirely built up with modern high-rise office buildings. The Metropolitan Opera House was razed in 1967 after the company had moved to its new house in Lincoln Center. Only small Greeley Square Park, retaining a portion of its original iron fence, remains from the 1893 photo. (9/12/74; 10:10.)

Broadway, North from West 40th Street (1912)

New York City's entertainment center gradually moved uptown until by 1912 it had spread along Broadway and its side streets from Herald Square to Times Square, continuing as far uptown as West 61st Street. When the Broadway Theatre was built in 1887 at the southwest corner of West 41st Street, it was one of the largest theaters in the city. Edwin Booth, Mrs. Leslie Carter and Blanche Bates were among the luminaries who played the Broadway. *Hanky Panky* featured Lew Fields of the famous Weber and Fields comedy team. After World War I the Broadway became a vaudeville and moving-picture house until it was demolished in 1929. The Times Building Tower, at 42nd Street, stands in the center of the photo. The Hotel Astor is beyond, at 44th Street. The square construction at the left of the Times Building is a tower, built in 1910, to back advertising signs. It stands on the site of George Considine's Metropole Hotel and Bar, for many years a popular rendezvous for the sporting and theatrical crowd until it was torn down in 1910. Just below the advertising tower is the six-story former Hotel Rossmore, built in 1873. In 1909 it was remodeled as the lavish Café de l'Opéra. In 1912 the well-known restaurateur Louis Martin renovated the building to house his new restaurant, the Café de Paris. It failed in 1913 and the building was gone by 1915. On the right, in front of the Hotel Albany, is a typical small Broadway movie theater marked by the sign "Motion Pictures."

Broadway, North from West 40th Street (1975)

Much of the entertainment in New York City continues to be centered around Times Square. All the many theaters that were built below 42nd Street are now gone, except one—the Billy Rose Theatre on West 41st Street (not visible). Only three buildings remain that were shown in the 1912 photo on the left (west) side of Broadway. They have been altered almost beyond recognition. On the site of the Broadway Theatre stands the 33-story Bricken-Textile Building at 1441 Broadway. Across 41st Street is the six-story building built for the Commercial Trust Co. in 1908. Enlarged another bay, heightened an extra two stories and stripped of its cornice and former classical entrance (1967), it is now an office building. In the middle of the block stands the 12-story former Brokaw Bros. Building (1915), now occupied by a savings and loan association. At the north end of the block, on the southwest corner of 42nd Street, is the seven-story Crossroads Building. It has lost its cornice, but not the ugly tower, visible above the roof of the savings and loan building. Across 42nd Street stands the former Times Tower, now the Expo America Tower. W. T. Grant's building, erected on the site of the Astor Hotel, overlooks the tower. In the center of the photo is the huge Uris Building at 50th Street, built on the site of the Capitol Theatre. (3/25/75; 10:50.)

West 42nd Street at Broadway, Looking West (1898)

Even before the New York entertainment center moved up from Herald Square, the northwest corner of Broadway and 42nd Street featured a giant billboard advertising theatrical attractions. Billboards were abundant and were permitted to be put up on old structures that were soon to be razed or reconstructed. Here we read that Clyde Fitch's *The Moth and the Flame* was playing at the Lyceum (Fourth Avenue and 24th Street). The American Theatre (42nd Street and Eighth Avenue) was featuring the Castle Square Opera Co., and *Way Down East* was playing. Brownstone houses stood on the north side of West 42nd Street between Seventh and Eighth Avenues. The square tower of St. Luke's Lutheran Church rose in the middle of the block. Transportation consisted of cable cars for Broadway and horsecars for 42nd Street plus the usual horse-drawn vehicles. The street cleaner, with his barrel on wheels, was a necessity to handle the horses' excrement.

Broadway and West 42nd Street, Looking Northwest (1903)

In 1898, a nine-story building, only 56 feet wide and a mere 25 feet in depth, was built for the Pabst Beer Co. of Milwaukee at the head of the triangle formed by the intersection of Broadway, West 42nd Street and Seventh Avenue. The building was known as the Pabst Hotel. Pabst's Bar and Restaurant occupied the first and second floors, with an elaborate extension over an open arcade on 42nd Street. The hotel was torn down in 1903. The four-story buildings which occupied the remainder of the triangle were demolished in 1902 during the construction of the new I.R.T. subway. In 1898, Oscar Hammerstein, the famous impresario, erected Hammerstein's Victoria, a large theater with a roof garden, on the northwest corner of Seventh Avenue and 42nd Street. It offered the highest quality vaudeville and minstrel shows. Playing at the time of the photo were the famous Primrose and Dockstader Minstrels. On the right, from 43rd to 44th Streets, stands a block of four-story residential buildings called the Barrington Apartments. Twenty-two years later the present Paramount Building was built on the site. This photo provides a good close-up of a tall type of gas street-light fixture, with footholds and protective glass globe, that was used at busy intersections.

In 1903 the architects Eidlitz and MacKenzie designed a handsome building, with a tower modeled on Giotto's campanile in Florence, for the *New York Times*. It was built in 1903-05 on the triangle at Broadway, West 42nd Street and Seventh Avenue. The area bounded by Broadway and Seventh Avenue from 43rd to 45th Streets, formerly the southern part of Longacre Square, was renamed Times Square. The building was occupied by the paper as its main office for less than eight years. In 1913 it moved to another fine new building on West 43rd Street. The north side of West 42nd Street, beyond Seventh Avenue, was going theatrical. Besides Hammerstein's Victoria, on the northwest corner, two adjoining theaters had been built: the Stuyvesant, which became the Belasco (later renamed the Republic and now the Victory)— where Blanche Bates was playing *The Girl of the Golden West*— and the entrance to the Lyric. At the extreme right is the Hotel Astor (designed by Clinton & Russell), the principal hotel of Times Square, completed in 1904.

Broadway and West 42nd Street, Looking Northwest (1906)

Broadway, West 42nd Street and Seventh Avenue,
Looking North to 43rd Street (1974)

The corner of Broadway and 42nd Street may no longer be the "busiest in the country" or the "crossroads of the world," but it is still one of the focal points of the city. In 1961 the Allied Chemical Co. took over the Times Tower and by 1964 had stripped it down to its steel skeleton. A new stone dressing and a completely new interior were built, thereby providing Allied Chemical with a new tower building. In 1974 it became the Expo America Tower. The famous Times news ribbon, with its moving headlines circling the building at the fourth-floor level, was retained, much to the public's satisfaction. Hammerstein's Victoria was entirely reconstructed in 1915 as a motion-picture house, known as the Rialto. It was torn down in 1935 and a new building was erected with two movie theaters, the Rialto and the Rialto Two. Rising up above the China Bowl sign on the left is the present New York Times building on West 43rd Street. On the right center is the Paramount Building, built in 1926. It contains stores and offices and once held one of the largest and most ornate moving-picture theaters ever built. Because of the lack of patronage and costly upkeep, the theater and lobbies were removed in 1966 and office space was substituted in their place. Beyond the Paramount Building rises the Grant Tower Building, built in 1972-74 on the site of the Hotel Astor. It contains the Minskoff, one of the new Broadway theaters. At the extreme right is the edge of the Uris Building (1970-71) with two theaters—the Uris and the Levine (renamed Circle in the Square). The old tradition of naming theaters after playwrights, producers and actors seems to have ended. (12/27/74; 10:35.)

East Side of Broadway, South from West 44th Street (1909)

This view shows the two most famous "lobster palaces" in New York—Rector's and Shanley's. Elsie Janis, who later entertained troups at the front during World War I, was playing in the musical *The Fair Co-ed* (book by George Ade) at the Criterion. In the southeast-corner office building, the Plaza Café on the ground floor and the upstairs tenants, including the songwriter and music publisher Gus Edwards, were all preparing to vacate. The signs on the second floor indicate that Charles Rector would very shortly build a 15-story hotel on this plot. The great Rector's Restaurant, with the giant illuminated griffin in front, flourished on Times Square with the backing of Diamond Jim Brady, known as the "King of the Great White Way." The eight-story Hotel Cadillac, originally the Barrett House when it was built in 1883 (Eugene O'Neill was born there in 1888), survived until 1940. Although very successful, Shanley's survived Rector's by only little more than a year, closing in 1911. The 14-story building with mansard roof (at the southeast corner of 42nd Street) is the Hotel Knickerbocker, built in 1904. It was the home of Enrico Caruso for many years and was also famous for the Maxwell Parrish mural of King Cole over its bar. In the center, a switchman has set up his little bench and umbrella against an elaborate street light, erected in the small island where Seventh Avenue intersects Broadway.

East Side of Broadway, South from West 44th Street (1975)

A two-story commercial building replaced the old Criterion Theatre in 1935. It included a new Criterion Theatre further north, near 45th Street. The Hotel Rector, built in 1910-11 at the southeast corner of 44th Street, bankrupted Charles Rector. In 1912 it became the Claridge and stood until 1972. The 33-story tower on the site, erected in 1972-74, and called the 1500 Broadway Building, occupies the entire block front. It contains a new movie theater, the National. The 12-story Fitzgerald Building was built on the southeast corner of 43rd Street in 1910. It included the George M. Cohan Theatre. In 1939 the building was demolished and a two-story business building, housing Toffenetti's Restaurant, was built there.

In 1968 it was taken over by Nathan's, the "Frankfurter King" of Coney Island fame. One of Times Square's elaborate lighted signs, six stories tall, occupies the roof. The 12-story former Longacre Building (1912) stands on the northeast corner of 42nd Street. The former Hotel Knickerbocker was altered into an office building in 1921. The Maxwell Parrish mural was transferred to the St. Regis Hotel. The 42-story Continental tower building was erected in 1930-31 at 41st Street. The top of the Empire State Building appears just right of center. A dividing mall with shrubbery has been added to Times Square. (3/25/75; 9:20.)

Broadway, Looking South from West 47th Street (1878)

Broadway was anything but glamorous around 47th Street. The street paving generally consisted of dirt with irregularly spaced cobblestones. Sidewalks were composed of flagstones of varying sizes. Traffic was light and the buildings were small, drab and unattractive. On the right (west side of Broadway), the marble works probably made columns, statuary and gravestones. Across the street are stables, a carpenter and a locksmith/bell hanger. On the southeast corner of West 47th Street is the small New Washington Market, where farmers and fishermen could bring and sell their produce without traveling miles downtown to the older and larger Washington Market. All the structures on the left were demolished by 1890, leaving an open triangle from Broadway to Seventh Avenue between 46th and 47th Streets. This became the northern end of Longacre Square, which extended down to 42nd Street. The area had been the city's carriage-trade center since Brewster & Co., famous carriage makers, moved to the west block from 47th Street to 48th Street (not visible) in 1872. The square took its name from Longacre, the carriage center in London. In less than 30 years this drab location would become an important part of the entertainment center of New York.

Broadway, Looking South from West 47th Street (1975)

While the southern part of Longacre Square was renamed Times Square in 1904, the designation of the northern section was not changed until 1939, when it was named Duffy Square after Father Francis Duffy (1871-1932) of the Fighting 69th Regiment of World War I. A statue of Duffy was set up here in 1937. A statue of showman George M. Cohan (1893-1942) was unveiled about 100 feet in front of Father Duffy in 1959. The Cohan statue can be seen directly above the car in the middle of Broadway. The low building marked "tkts" at the rear of Duffy Square is occupied by a ticket office where seats are sold for certain theatrical attractions at half-price. The 16-story building, left of center, with the *Great Gatsby* wall sign, is the Loew's State theater and office building (1920). The original theater (capacity 4400) was divided into two motion-picture theaters in 1968 by converting the former balcony into a second auditorium. The 33-story tower in the center is the 1500 Broadway office building, completed in 1974. In the right center of the photo, under the billboard lights, is the former Times Tower. (3/25/75; 10:15.)

East Side of Broadway, North from West 47th Street (1909)

Famous for the many elaborate electric commercial signs between 42nd and 53rd Streets, Broadway became known as "The Great White Way." Although several vacancies existed, the section on Broadway north of the upper part of Longacre Square (extreme right) was already beginning to develop. The ten-story office and store building at the northeast corner of 48th Street (built in 1904) was the first tall building in this area. The Studebaker sign on the roof and the tire signs on the low building show that the automobile trade was settling on Broadway from 47th to 59th Streets, already known as "Automobile Row." It supplanted the older carriage center.

East Side of Broadway, North from West 47th Street (1974)

Billboards and electric signs are still dominant on this part of Broadway, but the modern signs are larger than their old counterparts. The 70-year-old structure with the huge Sony sign, now known as the National Screen Service Building, remains with little change. In front of this building, at the southeast corner of 48th Street, is a two-story restaurant and night-club building. It was originally known as the Palais Royal, where the great bandleader Paul Whiteman made his debut. In succession it became the Cotton Club, Connie's Inn, the Latin Quarter, the Lido Night Club and finally the present Cine Lido, a movie house featuring "adult" films. The two skyscrapers rising on the right from Sixth Avenue are the McGraw-Hill Building at 48th Street and the Exxon Building at 49th Street, both completed in 1973. (12/7/74; 10:46.)

Broadway and Central Park West, Looking North from Columbus Circle (1899)

Grand Circle, the space where Broadway, Central Park West (Eighth Avenue) and Central Park South (West 59th Street) meet at the southwest corner of Central Park, was renamed Columbus Circle in 1894 to celebrate (two years late) the 400th anniversary of the discovery of America by the Italian explorer. On October 12 of that year an imposing monument, consisting of a tall column, with bronze reliefs of anchors and ships' prows, mounted on an impressive base and crowned with a statue of Columbus by Gaetano Russo, was unveiled and dedicated. Central Park West goes off to the north (right), while Broadway slants to the left. The two-story building on the triangular block where the two avenues meet was occupied by Durland's Riding Academy, then one of the largest equestrian schools in the world. At the northwest corner of Central Park West and West 61st Street, is the seven-story Poillon apartment house. In the distance, on the extreme right, at West 72nd Street, stands the 11-story Hotel Majestic, built in 1893-94. The large building on the far left, at the southwest corner of West 63rd Street and Broadway, is the Hotel Empire. From 66th Street to around 116th Street, Broadway was becoming a residential thoroughfare lined with apartment buildings. The passing streetcars are running on the Eighth Avenue line.

Broadway and Central Park West, Looking North from Columbus Circle (1975)

The Columbus Monument, with its original iron fence, stands unchanged. The setting has been improved by the addition of the 12 fountains surrounding it. The triangular site is occupied by the 44-story Gulf & Western Building, built in 1968-71. On Central Park West from West 61st to West 62nd Streets is the Mayflower Hotel, which replaced the Poillon apartment building in 1926. On the next block, from West 62nd to West 63rd Streets, the 30-story twin-towered Century apartment building, designed by Irwin S. Chanin in 1931, took the place of the Century Theatre, begun in 1907 as the New Theatre with Carrère & Hastings as architects. This theater, when opened in 1909, was considered one of the finest and most elaborate in the country. Further north along Central Park West are the tall twin towers of the Majestic apartment building (1930-31), also designed by Chanin. It

replaced the old Majestic Hotel. A corner of the New York Coliseum, where conventions and exhibitions are held, is visible at the left, at the southwest corner of Broadway and West 60th Street. Four blocks farther north, at the southwest corner of Broadway and West 63rd Street, is a second Hotel Empire, which replaced the first Empire Hotel in 1923. On the left, immediately beyond West 63rd Street, one can see a bit of two of the buildings which are part of vast Lincoln Center, where five buildings were built (1962-69) to house the performing arts. Across from Lincoln Center, on the right of Broadway at West 63rd Street, is the 43-story apartment and business building known as No. 1 Lincoln Plaza (1969-70). The Hotel Ansonia, at 73rd Street, is the building that appears in the far distance at the end of the vista down Broadway. (8/18/75; 1:30.)

Broadway, North from West 70th Street (1904)

Above 59th Street, Broadway becomes the principal thoroughfare of the upper West Side, lined with large apartment buildings, most with stores on the street level. In 1904 the I.R.T. subway opened. With attractive stations at each stop located in the center mall, it offered direct transportation to the entertainment, shopping and financial centers of the city. This view shows Sherman Square, where Broadway intersects Amsterdam Avenue. One of the very early sightseeing omnibuses (left) is ready to take off with a crowd. The ornate luxury apartment building on the right, at the 71st Street corner, is the Dorilton (Janes & Leo,

architects), built in 1901. From 70th to 71st Streets, on the left, is the Sherman Square Hotel, built in two entirely different sections. On the next corner stands Christ Church (1889), the second oldest Episcopal parish in the city (organized in 1794). Just beyond the church is the Colonial Club building at 72nd Street. At the northwest corner of 72nd Street is the eight-story Hotel St. Andrew. The 17-story Ansonia is in the center of the photo, between 73rd and 74th Streets. When it was built in 1899-1904 by W. E. D. Stokes, owner and part architect, the Ansonia was considered the largest and most elaborate apartment hotel in the world.

Broadway, North from West 70th Street (1975)

Broadway remains the principal artery of the upper West Side. Benches and concrete traffic guards have been added to the center mall. Behind the bench on the mall is the same iron-spike fence placed there 71 years ago to protect the I.R.T. subway station ventilator. On the extreme right is the 17-story former Hotel Alamac. Across 71st Street the Dorilton stands with little change. The Sherman Square Hotel was replaced in 1970 by the present 42-story apartment building with its entrance at 201 West 70th Street. Christ Church sold its Broadway frontage in 1925, and an office building was erected. The church continues to use the remainder of the old church building, part of which is visible. The former Colonial Club building at 72nd Street, seen to the left of the center lamppost, is now an office building. The Hotel St. Andrew, demolished in 1938, was replaced by a two-story business building. The Ansonia, minus the ornate cupolas formerly on the top of the corner towers, is now an apartment building with many residents from the musical and theatrical world. It has been designated a city landmark. (3/11/75; 11:18.)

The Boulevard (Broadway), South from West 114th Street (1895)

The old Bloomingdale Road was one of the main roads leading out of Manhattan, running through from Union Square up to Westchester County. The road was gradually absorbed by Broadway as far as 59th Street. In 1867 an extension north from 59th Street to 125th Street was laid out with a generous mall in the center and with a double row of trees and wide sidewalks. It was known simply as the Boulevard until 1899, when Broadway was extended to 168th Street. This photo shows the Boulevard as it appeared before construction started on the I.R.T. subway in 1902. In 1884 the 42nd Street, Manhattanville and St. Nicholas Railway Co. was granted a franchise to operate a horsecar line on Broadway and the Boulevard from 42nd to 125th Streets. The wide Boulevard, with little traffic, was fine for bicycling, which enjoyed a vogue until automobile traffic made it impracticable. Most of the construction on this section of Broadway was spurred by Columbia University's move to the area in 1897 and by the completion of the I.R.T. subway in 1904.

Broadway, South from West 114th Street (1975)

The tree-lined mall still gives Broadway north of 59th Street a distinction that other New York streets do not have, except possibly Park Avenue. With Riverside Park only one block west, and with good transportation and shopping, this section of Broadway is a popular residential area. Many of these apartment buildings on both sides of Broadway, averaging 12 to 15 stories in height, were built between 1907 and 1915. From 110th to 116th Streets, shops, restaurants and bars cater to the thousands of Columbia students. The seven-story building that formerly housed the St. Luke's Home for Aged Women (built 1897-99) is on the extreme left. The home, now known as Morningside House, moved to the Bronx in 1974. (3/18/75; 12:05.)

Manhattan Street (West 125th Street), Looking East toward Broadway (1903)

Broadway dips into the Manhattanville Valley between 120th and 135th Streets, the lowest point being at 125th Street (originally named Manhattan Street). In order to maintain a proper grade on the I.R.T. subway, the three tracks emerge from the tunnel at 122nd Street, cross the valley on a steel viaduct and reenter the tunnel at 135th Street. When this photo was taken on July 10, 1903, the roadbed, the 71-foot-high steel arch and the station platforms were under construction. Note the steam hoist (right) on the viaduct. The station house itself was built on the ground with escalators reaching the train platforms. On the busy street below the viaduct are electric cars of the 125th Street crosstown line on the center tracks and horsecars of the 110th Street crosstown line on the outer tracks. There are two types of city rubbish collection wagons in this photo: the metal type on the right and the older wooden kind alongside the horsecar. Beyond the viaduct, the development of 125th Street as the main business street of Harlem is noticeable. A poster on the left advertises *The Wizard of Oz*, a musical adaptation of L. Frank Baum's tale that was enjoying a run at the Majestic Theatre on Columbus Circle. A sign on the right recommends the use of "Aunt Hannah's Death Drops."

West 125th Street, Looking East toward Broadway (1975)

There have been few changes on the viaduct: the upper platforms have been enclosed and the waiting room has been moved from street level to the area marked by the windows just below the tracks. A large billboard has been suspended near the center of the arch and a siren is placed on the platform roof. West 125th Street is quite drab and colorless in the vicinity of Broadway, although some commercial buildings and walk-up apartment houses have been built since 1903. Except for one of the modern high-rise apartment buildings of the General Grant Houses (right, beyond the viaduct) there has been little urban renewal in the immediate area. The two-story commercial building with the second-floor bowling alley (right) stands as a burnt-out shell with no sign of repairs. The storage building seen in the distance at the center of the 1903 photo still stands. (3/18/75; 11:35.)

Fifth Avenue, North from 8th Street (1898)

The fine residential atmosphere of Fifth Avenue, with its wide sidewalks, provided a suitable setting for the leisurely pace of 1898. It was a cold, sunny day when a mother, her bundled child in a wicker baby carriage, prepared to cross the avenue. The photo offers a fairly close look at the famous hansom cab, named for its designer, J. A. Hansom, who patented the design in England in 1834. New York City did not see them until after 1890.

Fifth Avenue, North from 8th Street (1974)

Lower Fifth Avenue continues to attract strollers along its tree-lined sidewalk, but the baby in this photo is being carried rather than wheeled. This section of the avenue remains residential, but apartment houses have replaced the mansions of last century. Only three of the buildings in the 1898 photo remain. The one on the extreme left is one of these, and the building with the fire escape incorporates two of the older buildings (built in 1848-49 by Henry Brevoort), with a renovated front in place of their original Gothic Revival facades. (10/7/74; 10:30.)

Fifth Avenue, Looking North from East 10th Street (1899)

This view gives some of the feeling of the elegance and wealth of Fifth Avenue in the nineteenth century. Here we see the wide stone-slab sidewalks before the removal of the front yards , the handsome private homes (which later lost their stoops) and two of Manhattan's outstanding churches. Nearest, at the northwest corner of West 10th Street, is the Episcopal Church of the Ascension. Designed by Richard Upjohn (the architect of Trinity Church), it was the first church built on Fifth Avenue (1840-41). Four years later the First Presbyterian Church was built on the block between West 11th and West 12th Streets; architect Joseph C. Wells modeled the tower on that of Magdalen College at Oxford, England. Commercial buildings have begun their intrusion further up the avenue.

Fifth Avenue, Looking North from East 10th Street (1974)

The two venerable churches remain, but the grand old residences of lower Fifth Avenue are gone. Automobiles and buses fill the avenue, detracting from its former quiet, calm and dignified atmosphere. From 12th Street to 59th Street, public and office buildings line Fifth Avenue. The Empire State Building, the world's tallest building for 41 years after its opening in 1931, towers at Fifth Avenue and 34th Street. (10/7/74; 10:50.)

Fifth Avenue, Looking North from West 14th Street (1899)

The corner building was originally the William M. Halstead residence, built in the 1830s. One of the earliest mansions on the avenue, it was later altered and became, successively, the Old Guard Armory, Midget Hall and Brewster's Hall; it eventually was occupied by the Gregg Furniture Co. Note the old-style fire hydrant across 14th Street and the rare and fancy street designator and stanchion at the right. This photo provides a close-up of Fifth Avenue's early electric streetlights and lampposts.

Fifth Avenue, Looking North from West 14th Street (1974)

Here we see the business thoroughfare that this section of lower Fifth Avenue became from 12th Street to 59th Street in the years between 1888 and 1910. (10/7/74; 10:55.)

Fifth Avenue, Looking North from East 16th Street (1890)

The large building at the northwest corner of Fifth Avenue and West 16th Street (Judge Building) was built in 1888, the year of New York's great blizzard. It was designed by McKim, Mead and White for the publisher Mrs. Frank Leslie, and became the home of the famous humor magazine *Judge* and *Frank Leslie's Illustrated Newspaper*, also housing Fischer Pianos and several printing firms. This building was one of the earliest large business structures to start the transformation of Fifth Avenue into a commercial street. Another 1888 building stands four blocks further uptown, at the southwest corner of West 20th Street, to the left of the church spire. For many years this building was the headquarters of the Methodist Book Concern, then the oldest publishing house in America. The spire is part of the South Dutch Reformed Church, built in 1849 at the southwest corner of West 21st Street. A Fifth Avenue stagecoach moves downtown. Trunks are being delivered in the wagon on 16th Street.

Fifth Avenue, Looking North from East 16th Street (1974)

The former Judge Building still stands at Fifth Avenue and West 16th Street, but its front has been mutilated by tasteless alterations. The few additions to the former Methodist Book Concern have not changed its character. The freestanding curved-top mailbox has gradually taken the place of the smaller mailbox that used to hang on lampposts and poles. (10/2/74; 11:10.)

Fifth Avenue, North from 22nd Street (1889)

Crossing Fifth Avenue at 22nd Street is a finely turned-out brougham carriage with a well-dressed driver and sleek horses. Imposing trees still survive on the avenue. On the extreme right is the six-story Glenham Hotel, built about 1875. On the northeast corner of 22nd Street stands the former St. Germain Hotel (1855), later the Cumberland apartment house. It sports the sign of the New York Jockey Club on its third-floor railing. There are six commercial buildings on the left. The first three are former dwellings, while the light-colored six-story building with cast-iron front is occupied by the noted furrier C. G. Gunther. The adjacent corner building was erected in 1883 for the Western Union Telegraph Co. Looking up Fifth Avenue, we see the trees of Madison Square Park on the right and the renowned Fifth Avenue Hotel on the left. Just beyond the hotel, at the point where Broadway crosses Fifth Avenue, stands the granite obelisk dedicated in 1858 over the grave of Major General William Jenkins Worth, a hero of the Mexican War.

Fifth Avenue, North from 22nd Street (1975)

The former Glenham Hotel, now a commercial building, has suffered little change. The Cumberland apartment building, along with several small buildings located in the triangle formed by 22nd Street, Fifth Avenue and Broadway, was demolished in 1900 to make way for the famous Flatiron Building. Of the six business buildings on the left side of the block from 22nd to 23rd Streets, three are practically unchanged; the other three have been torn down or renovated beyond recognition. The 23-foot-wide corner apartment building at the extreme left was built in 1922. It is a bit isolated in this business district. The 14-story, block long Fifth Avenue Office Building has replaced the Fifth Avenue Hotel, but the Worth Monument remains. The Empire State Building at 34th Street and the 500 Fifth Avenue Building at 42nd Street are the two towers rising up on the west side of the avenue and dominating the skyline. (3/3/75; 9:40.)

Junction of Broadway and Fifth Avenue, South from West 24th Street (1889)

The meeting of the two principal streets of the city forms an apex known as the "cowcatcher." At the extreme left is the seven-story Hotel Bartholdi. Madison Square Park (not visible) is located on the left. In 1884 the Western Union Telegraph Co. built one of the earliest commercial buildings on Fifth Avenue; it stands on the right, at the southwest corner of West 23rd Street. It was designed by Henry J. Hardenbergh, who in that year had completed the Dakota, one of the early apartment buildings in the city. The second Plaza Hotel (1907) was also designed by Hardenbergh. The six-story building on the extreme right is the Fifth Avenue Hotel (1858), the most famous and fashionable of its day. It could accommodate a thousand guests and had the first passenger elevator (then called a vertical railway car) in New York. The photo shows various modes of transportation—wagon, horsecar, stagecoach and horseback.

Junction of Broadway and Fifth Avenue, South from West 24th Street (1974)

Broadway and Fifth Avenue are now both busy commercial streets. The 20-story Fuller Building, built in 1901-02, popularly known as the Flatiron Building, occupies the "cowcatcher" site. Its height was made possible by steel-frame construction. On the right, the former Western Union Telegraph Building remains at the 23rd Street corner. Besides two altered old brownstones in the center of the Fifth Avenue block between 23rd and 22nd Streets, the six-story brownstone business building on East 22nd Street, in back of the Flatiron Building, still stands. The Fifth Avenue Hotel was demolished in 1908 and in its place rose the present 14-story Fifth Avenue Office Building (right), which still maintains a fine-looking sidewalk clock. One of the older Fifth Avenue street lamps has been left standing at the apex of the Flatiron Building triangle. (9/30/74; 12:05.)

49

Fifth Avenue, Looking South from East 34th Street (1894)

William Waldorf Astor had recently completed the tall Hotel Waldorf at the northwest corner of West 33rd Street on the site of his former residence. John Jacob Astor, William's cousin, whose mansion stands on the right at the West 34th Street corner, would soon follow his cousin's lead and erect the much larger Astoria Hotel; together, these were to form the famous Waldorf-Astoria. The six-story Hotel Cambridge is at the southwest corner of West 33rd Street. In the center of the photo, the spire of the Marble Collegiate Reformed Church at West 29th Street, completed in 1854, appears behind the flag of the Holland House Hotel, on the northwest corner of West 30th Street. Although the conversion of Fifth Avenue into a commercial street had already begun, a good number of residences, with their front stoops, still remain. The electric streetlights were recent additions.

Fifth Avenue, Looking South from East 34th Street (1974)

Various landmarks still remain, including the spire of the Marble Collegiate Reformed Church and the former Holland House Hotel, both visible in the center of the photo. The last-named building was renovated for office use in 1920. In 1925 the Hotel Cambridge was replaced by the 14-story office building just south of the Empire State Building at 33rd Street. On the right center, the structure with the wide overhanging cornice at the northwest corner of West 32nd Street is the former Reed & Barton Building, built in 1904. The differences between the design of the present streetlights and those of 80 years ago are apparent. (9/12/74; 9:25.)

Fifth Avenue, Looking North from 33rd Street (1905)

The Waldorf-Astoria stands on the left. Across 34th Street is Stanford White's Knickerbocker Trust Co. On the right, Benjamin Altman had begun construction of the steel framework of his store at the southeast corner of Fifth Avenue and East 35th Street. He planned the store for the entire block south to 34th Street and east to Madison Avenue, but it was another five years before he secured control of the northeast corner of 34th Street, then occupied by the brownstone Knoedler Art Gallery. On the right, two blocks beyond Altman's is the new six-story Tiffany Store Building at the southeast corner of East 37th Street. On the left, at West 36th Street, the structure with the wide overhanging cornice is the recently completed Gorham Building. The steeple of the Brick Presbyterian Church, built in 1858, stands prominently at the northwest corner of West 37th Street. Many hansom cabs are visible but only one automobile is in sight (in front of the Knickerbocker Trust Co. at 34th Street corner; the first mass-produced car in the nation was the 1902 Oldsmobile).

Fifth Avenue, Looking North from 33rd Street (1974)

The marble-fronted Altman store stands completed. The Waldorf-Astoria Hotel was demolished in 1929 and the Empire State Building was erected on the site. The Knickerbocker Trust building has been enlarged and altered beyond recognition. The former Gorham Building at West 36th Street remains, but the Brick Presbyterian Church was demolished in 1938. The 58-story No. 500 Fifth Avenue, on the northwest corner of 42nd Street, was the seventh tallest structure in the city when built in 1930. (9/12/74; 9:35.)

West Side of Fifth Avenue, Looking North to West 34th Street (1899)

Full long skirts, short jackets and fancy hats perched high on ample hair was the style seen on Fifth Avenue in 1899. Here two ladies demonstrate the "skirt clutch" used to keep skirts from being dirtied on the street. The wide sidewalks of the "Queen of Avenues," especially alongside the elegant and imposing Waldorf-Astoria Hotel, were popular for strollers who came to see and be seen. The avenue boasted New York's wealthiest and most impressive residences (such as A. T. Stewart's marble mansion, a bit of which is visible at the northwest corner of 34th Street), and the best club buildings, the leading churches, the finest hotels and, before very long, the best stores.

West Side of Fifth Avenue, Looking North to West 34th Street (1974)

The Empire State Building took the place of the Waldorf-Astoria Hotel in 1931. Fifth Avenue is now commercial, but it remains the most famous and exciting avenue in New York. Its pace has quickened and window shopping is a favorite pastime for pedestrians, the displays being the most creative, attractive and enterprising in the nation. (12/6/74; 12:15.)

(1875)

(1912)

(1974)

West 34th Street, Looking West from Fifth Avenue

(1875)

Cobblestoned West 34th Street was a quiet residential street in 1875. The brownstone mansion with the elaborate bay window (right) was the home of Prescott H. Butler. In later years it was occupied by the Knoedler Art Gallery. A. T. Stewart, pioneer merchant in New York City, built his million-dollar five-story marble residence on the northwest corner of Fifth Avenue in 1868, but lived in it for only eight years. It was torn down in 1903, having been occupied by the Manhattan Club for ten years. The Broadway Tabernacle Church (1859-1905) stands out prominently at the northeast corner of 34th Street and Sixth Avenue. Beyond that are the pinnacles of the B'nai Jeshurun Synagogue, located west of Broadway, on part of the site of the future R. H. Macy store building. Finally, on the left, just west of Eighth Avenue, is the tall square tower of the Thirty-Fourth Street Dutch Reformed Church.

(1912)

By 1912, the corner of Fifth Avenue and West 34th Street was solidly built up with commercial buildings. The large building on the far left is the McCreery department store. The bank on the corner, designed by Stanford White for the Knickerbocker Trust Co., stands on the site of the Stewart mansion. It later became the Columbia Trust Co. White skillfully adapted the classical forms—Corinthian pilasters and three-quarter columns, elaborately carved frieze, handsome cornice and balustrade—to a four-story bank building.

(1974)

West 34th Street has become one of the busiest shopping streets in New York. Ohrbach's has taken the place of McCreery's (the wide building with balconies, just left of center) and many large and small store and office buildings dominate the street. The handsome bank disappeared when the Columbia Trust Co. added ten stories in 1920. When the building was further modernized in 1962, all traces of the once outstanding classical facade were removed. The adjoining 12-story office building to the west has had a "face lift" on its exterior. Under the misapprehension that it improves appearances, many owners spend millions each year mutilating older facades in the name of modernization. Macy's is identified by the large "M" on the side of its Seventh Avenue wing. Beyond that is the 45-story Nelson tower (1931) at Seventh Avenue. (9/12/74; 10:05.)

East Side of Fifth Avenue, North from 35th Street (1907)

Five hansom cabs and a buggy comprise the traffic on Fifth Avenue. One automobile is on East 35th Street, parked at a right angle to the curb facing B. Altman's. Of the eight buildings on the east block from 35th to 36th Street, three brownstone residences remain untouched; another has been leveled, and a new commercial building is under construction on the site; and four are already business buildings. The Alvin Building (1905), at the northeast corner of 35th Street, is one of the new imposing office buildings. It has a 25-foot frontage on the avenue. In the center of the photo, at the southeast corner of East 37th Street, is the Tiffany Building (1905), designed by Stanford White in the style of the Palazzo Grimani of Venice (1539). Another early office building, which stands out prominently two blocks north of the Tiffany Building, is the 11-story Knabe Piano Building (1904), at the southern corner of East 39th Street. This building is an impressive example of Beaux-Arts architecture.

East Side of Fifth Avenue, North from 35th Street (1975)

Not a single private residence now stands as far north as East 61st Street. The Alvin Building and its adjoining neighbor remain with little change, save the usual street-front mutilation. The 15-story building at the southeast corner of East 36th Street was built in 1929 by Henry Mandel. The former Tiffany Building was altered for general office use in 1951 but retains its exterior. Beyond it, across East 37th Street, stands a 1915 terra-cotta and stucco office building. Adjoining it to the north is the 11-story former Bonwit-Teller Building (1911). The former Knabe Building is just about noticeable behind the modern street lamp on the left. The tall modern structure, only four window-banks deep, is a recently completed office building at 487 Fifth Avenue, near 42nd Street. (11/20/75; 2:05.)

Fifth Avenue and 42nd Street, Looking North (1898)

The pace was leisurely, with bicycles, horsecars, broughams and hansom cabs comprising the traffic. The six-story building on the extreme right (No. 503, built about 1870) was the former residence of the banker and former governor of New York, Levi P. Morton. By 1887 the house—raised an extra story, with a large rear extension being added on 42nd Street—had been converted into the Hotel Meurice. In 1895 it became a commercial building. The twin Moorish towers belong to Temple Emanu-El, built 1868, at East 43rd Street.

At East 44th Street is the famous restaurant, Delmonico's, built in 1897. On the northwest corner of West 42nd Street stands the seven-story Hotel Bristol (1875). The ten-story building with the heavy cornice at West 44th Street is Louis Sherry's Restaurant Building—competition for Delmonico's across the avenue. A sidewalk merchant operates with a white makeshift awning (extreme left). The open horsecar is the 42nd Street crosstown line on the way to the North (Hudson) River and the ferry to Weehawken, New Jersey.

Fifth Avenue and 42nd Street, Looking North (1974)

Crowds and traffic have increased with the many tall office buildings in the Grand Central area, which copes daily with large numbers of office workers, sightseers and shoppers. Because of the heavy traffic, the first permanent traffic signal tower was built in the middle of Fifth Avenue, just north of 42nd Street, in 1922. It lasted until 1929, when corner signal lights were adopted. The former Morton residence is still going strong after over 100 years of activity. Such curious remnants are not uncommon in New York. Most of the office buildings on this part of Fifth Avenue were erected between 1907 and 1916. The 40-story Lefcourt National Building replaced the Temple Emanu-El in 1928. Delmonico's was demolished in 1926 and the 36-story Delmonico Building, now known as 535 Fifth Avenue, was built on the site. The former Hotel Bristol was removed in 1929, to be replaced by the 500 Fifth Avenue Building. (12/10/74; 1:20.)

Fifth Avenue, North from West 45th Street (1886)

The outstanding midtown hotel on Fifth Avenue was the Hotel Windsor, occupying the east side of the avenue from 46th to 47th Streets. It was built in 1873 when Fifth Avenue was a handsome residential street. On March 17, 1899, during the St. Patrick's Day parade, fire broke out on the seventh floor, resulting in the death of over 30 persons and the destruction of the building. Further up the avenue on the east side, the twin spires of St. Patrick's Cathedral are being completed. The tall brownstone steeple at the northwest corner of West 48th Street (left) belongs to the Collegiate Church of St. Nicholas, oldest church organization in America (1628). Built in 1871-72, it was demolished in 1949 to make way for an office building.

Fifth Avenue, North from West 45th Street (1974)

The only structure surviving from the 1886 cityscape is St. Patrick's Cathedral, whose spires are silhouetted against the 40-story Olympic Tower, nearing completion at the northeast corner of East 51st Street. All other buildings that can be seen in this photo were erected after 1900. At the southeast corner of East 46th Street is the modern office building 555 Fifth Avenue. The block between East 46th and 47th Streets, where the Windsor Hotel stood, is now occupied by the S. W. Straus Building (1921), altered in 1939 for general office use. On the far half of the block, at 47th Street, stands the eight-story W. & J. Sloane Building (1912), converted to Korvette's department store in 1962. Seventy-six years after the disastrous Windsor Hotel fire, a fire engine on the west side of the avenue has answered to a call from the Seaman's Savings Bank (corner of 45th Street), where some smoke is noticeable. (11/27/74, 12:30.)

It is Easter Sunday and practically everyone is out to see or be seen. The two-way street traffic is solid with hansom cabs, carriages, a bicycle and the automobile, which is rapidly taking the place of the horse. There are sedans, touring cars, limousines, open-top buses and even an early electric brougham at the lower left. The silk topper and the swallowtail coat are still in fashion. The derby and cap are in style for motoring. At the right, there are still three private homes, separated by a new six-story business building under construction at No. 605. At the northeast corner of East 49th Street is the eight-story Belgravia apartment house. The other two tall buildings on the block are the Hotel Buckingham, with its main entrance on East 50th Street, while between them is a four-story brownstone occupied by the National Democratic Club. Beyond St. Patrick's Cathedral is the three-story Union Club. The St. Regis Hotel (1904) at East 55th Street is the tall building at the far left.

East Side of Fifth Avenue, Looking North from West 48th Street (1912)

East Side of Fifth Avenue, Looking North from West 48th Street (1975)

The Scribner Building (right, behind the Bilkays truck) was designed in 1913 by Ernest Flagg. The second building to the left of Scribner's is a former private residence, converted to business use in 1914. On the southeast corner of East 49th Street stands the previous McCutcheon Store Building, built in 1924, used entirely as an office building since 1959. In 1923, Saks & Co. secured the entire block front from 49th to 50th Streets for Saks Fifth Avenue. The twin spires of St. Patrick's Cathedral are reflected in the glass wall of the Olympic Tower. Although the lower part of this structure will be used for shops and office space, it is the first residential building to go up on Fifth Avenue between 15th and 62nd Streets in more than 50 years. The mansard roof of the St. Regis Hotel is just visible to the left of the hanging traffic light. (6/9/75; 1:00.)

West 59th Street (Central Park South), Looking West from Fifth Avenue (1900)

The open space around West 59th Street at the southeast corner entrance to Central Park is officially called Grand Army Plaza, but is generally known simply as "the Plaza." The fine hotel facing onto it was also named the Plaza. This eight-story Plaza Hotel was built in 1887-90; started by the architects Fife & Campbell, it was completed by McKim, Mead and White. The first real development of the Plaza space came in 1903, when the handsome equestrian statue of General William T. Sherman by Augustus Saint-Gaudens was erected at the north end (not visible in the photo). West 59th Street, with its wide, ample sidewalk along the park, had developed into a desirable residential street. The first large group of eight apartment houses to be built as a unified structure, called the Navarro Flats, was erected in 1885 at the southeast corner of Seventh Avenue. Extending through to West 58th Street, it is the large building with the cone-shaped tower, to the right of center in the photo. In 1897 the New York Athletic Club built a large eight-story clubhouse at the southeast corner of Sixth Avenue and 59th Street; it is visible here to the left of the termination of the Sixth Avenue "el" at the center of the photo. The East Belt Line horsecar, on its way to First Avenue to start out on its route to South Ferry, is followed by a recently electrified cable car of the 59th Street crosstown line.

Central Park South, Looking West from Fifth Avenue (1975)

59th Street is the dividing line between commercial and residential Fifth Avenue. The stretch of West 59th Street from Fifth Avenue to Columbus Circle is now called Central Park South. Because of its location on the park, the street has become a popular high-rise apartment and hotel thoroughfare. The Grand Army Plaza was completely rebuilt and beautified in 1915. On the left stands one of the great hotels of the country—the second Plaza. The original Plaza Hotel was demolished in 1906 to make way for Henry Hardenbergh's 18-story Park Plaza Hotel, as it was then called. It was opened in 1907 as the world's most luxurious hotel, and for almost seven decades has maintained its reputation. Beyond the park, on the right, rises the 44-story Gulf & Western office building. The vicinity of the Grand Army Plaza continues to be the stand for open or closed carriages, and has become a favored site for frankfurter carts. (8/18/75; 11:00.)

East Side of Fifth Avenue, North from 112th Street (1902)

Traffic was light and the remains of the last snowfall were still in the street when this photo was taken of Fifth Avenue in Harlem. The character of Fifth Avenue changed north of 110th Street. It had been built up in the 1890s with blocks of five-story walk-up apartments. Land was available and cheaper beyond Central Park, especially between 110th Street and Mount Morris Park at 120th Street. Before the Harlem district was fully developed around World War I, it was practically a separate community or suburb with its own group of churches, theaters and shopping centers, which made it unnecessary for Harlem residents to travel to mid-Manhattan for their necessities. Fifth Avenue's monotonous rows of flats extend as far as Mount Morris Park, on the extreme left, which occupied four blocks of the avenue. In the park, appearing above the roof of the last apartment building, stands an old fire tower (1855, attributed to James Bogardus), one of the last relics of the days of New York's volunteer firemen.

East Side of Fifth Avenue, North from 112th Street (1975)

Many of Harlem's older walk ups have been demolished and replaced by modern high-rise apartment houses, such as the Senator Robert Taft Housing Development (right). Built in the area from 112th to 115th Streets and from Fifth to Park Avenues, it is composed of four 19-story buildings. Visible on the left is part of another new housing development, the Martin Luther King, Jr., Towers. Some of the older apartments remain on Fifth Avenue above 115th Street, and the old fire tower, now a city landmark, still rises above the roof of the last apartment on the right-hand side. Mount Morris Park has been renamed Marcus Garvey Park. There is now street traffic and parking and, as in 1902, the streets are not without snow. (3/18/75; 10:10.)

Lexington Avenue, North from East 59th Street (1912)

In 1912, this section of Lexington Avenue was rapidly becoming a busy location because two surface lines crossed here and it was near the entrance to the Queensboro Bridge. The area also boasted Gerstle's Café (as saloons were then known) and Bloomingdale's Department Store, which had expanded from its Third Avenue store with a 40-foot frontage on Lexington Avenue. The East Side I.R.T. subway did not operate to 59th Street until 1918, but indications of subway construction are already noticeable: waterpipes can be seen at the street curbs and there is a work building erected on a temporary bridge over the avenue at East 63rd Street. Painlessness, a fairly recent innovation in dentistry, is prominently advertised.

Lexington Avenue, North from East 59th Street (1974)

Lexington Avenue and East 59th Street has become one of the busiest corners in New York. The streetcar lines have been replaced by buses. Two subway systems cross at 60th Street and, in 1965, an express stop was added to accommodate the crowds. A modern bank building has taken over the northwest corner, and the new Bloomingdale's store building (1930) fills the entire block. Above 61st Street, Lexington Avenue continues to hold a residential character, with stores a secondary feature. (10/10/74; 12:15.)

Fourth Avenue, Looking North from the Junction with Third Avenue at East 6th Street (1893)

Triangular Cooper Park, where Third and Fourth Avenues meet in Cooper Square, makes an attractive setting for the brownstone Cooper Union Building, built 1853-59 by Peter Cooper as a free school for the advancement of science and art. This is the oldest building in the country framed with rolled structural steel beams—a forerunner of today's skyscraper. Three stories were added to the original five-story building in 1880-95; construction was under way on the seventh floor, right side, when this photo was taken. In 1860, in the Great Hall, an auditorium in the Union's basement, Abraham Lincoln delivered a speech that started him on the road to the Presidency. Standing directly behind Cooper Union, on the block bounded by Third and Fourth Avenues and East 8th and 9th Streets, is the six-story Bible House, built in 1852. On Third Avenue, at the extreme right, is a corner of the Tompkins Market and Armory Building (with sloping roof), which was erected for the 7th Regiment in 1860. Its first floor was used as a market. From 1880 until 1906 it housed the 69th Regiment. Across East 7th Street on Third Avenue is the Metropolitan Savings Bank (1867), built in the French style with a mansard roof. It was one of the first fireproof commercial buildings. The train on the Third Avenue elevated is just leaving the 9th Street station for downtown Manhattan.

Fourth Avenue, Looking North from the Junction with Third Avenue at East 6th Street (1975)

In 1897 the citizens of New York City honored Peter Cooper by dedicating a statue of him by Augustus Saint-Gaudens. Placed in an architectural setting by Stanford White, the statue stands in front of the Cooper Union Building. Now a city landmark, Cooper Union survives with little exterior change except for the extended round elevator tower on the roof. The original elevator cab was round, but it was replaced by the usual square cab. During the recent reconstruction, the round cab was restored. The Bible House was torn down in 1959. Cooper Union opened the School of Engineering and Science on the site in 1961. Rising up in the distance on the left is the 14th Street tower of the Consolidated Edison building. The Tompkins Market and Armory building was demolished in 1911 to make way for the Cooper Union School of Art and Architecture. Known as the Abram S. Hewitt Memorial, it is now used by the school for general activities. The former Metropolitan Savings Bank building has a reconstructed Third Avenue entrance; the roof cresting and flagpole have been removed. Now a city landmark, the building is occupied by the First Ukrainian Assembly of God. (5/8/75; 2:30.)

Fourth Avenue, Looking North from East 17th Street (1901)

The buildings on the left are facing the northeast corner of Union Square, which in 1901 was a pleasant park, not a popular place for outdoor protest meetings. The five-story building at the northwest corner of East 17th Street is the Everett House. Built in 1854, this hotel was convenient to 14th Street's shopping, musical and theatrical attractions. The Everett particularly attracted theatrical and professional people. To the left is the Century Building, the home of both the *Century* magazine, an outstanding literary publication, and the *St. Nicholas* magazine, the distinguished and popular publication for young people. The narrow 11-story office building at the far left is the Jackson Building. Behind the hotel, on the right, is the Bradley office building. The 13-story structure at the 19th Street corner houses the complete color-printing plant of the American Lithographic Company. The food vendor's cart alongside the Everett House is similar to those in use in New York today.

Park Avenue South (Fourth Avenue), Looking North from East 16th Street (1974)

The Everett House was replaced in 1908 by the Everett Building, now known as 200 Park Avenue South. The former Century Building remains, but a two-story business structure has recently been built on the site of the former Jackson Building. The nine-story Bradley Building remains, but its main cornice has been removed. The conical tower lifting its head at the extreme right belongs to the New York Life Insurance Building at 26th Street and Madison Avenue. (12/6/74; 12:10.)

West Side of Fourth Avenue, Looking North from East 21st Street (1895)

Leading directly to the Grand Central Station (then the only railroad station in Manhattan), Fourth Avenue was an important transportation artery. The two center horsecar tracks were used by the Fourth & Madison Avenue lines. The 42nd Street & Grand Street Ferry line utilized the right outer track on its way uptown to the Weehawken Ferry. At the northeast corner of East 21st Street is the brownstone front of Calvary Episcopal Church, designed by James Renwick and completed in 1846. Just beyond the church a corner tower of the Church Missions' House is visible. The handsome three-story white building on the southwest corner of East 22nd Street is the Bank for Savings (1894). It was designed by

C. L. W. Eidlitz. Founded in 1819, it is the oldest savings bank in New York State. Across 22nd Street, at the northwest corner, stands the Fourth Avenue Presbyterian Church. The southwest corner at 23rd Street is occupied by the five-story Y.M.C.A. On the northwest corner is P. B. Wright's National Academy of Design, built in the Venetian Gothic style in 1862. Three blocks farther north stand the two towers marking the rear section of Stanford White's Madison Square Garden. Its main tower appears over the Y.M.C.A. The white marble building under construction (upper left) is an addition to the Metropolitan Life Insurance Building on the south side of East 24th Street.

West Side of Park Avenue South (Fourth Avenue),
Looking North from East 21st Street (1975)

Embellished with a central mall planted with shrubs and trees, Fourth Avenue from 17th to 32nd Streets was renamed Park Avenue South in 1959. Calvary Church and the corner stone tower of the former Church Missions' House (now the Protestant Welfare Agencies building) remain. All the older structures on the west side of the avenue are gone, save the three-story Bank for Savings building, which remains with an alteration at the far corner of the building and a 1933 addition on the 22nd Street side (not visible). At the northwest corner of East 22nd Street, the 14-story former Mills & Gibb Building (now known as the 300 Park Avenue South Building) took the place of the Fourth Avenue Presbyterian Church. The Y.M.C.A. was demolished in 1903 to make way for Clinton & Russell's 11-story Mercantile Building. The Academy of Design building was demolished in 1901. The site was used by the expanding Metropolitan Life Insurance Co., which completed its building on the block from 23rd to 24th Streets, back to Madison Avenue, by 1909. The company modernized the structure by completely renovating it in 1954-55. The tall, massive 27-story building dressed in light stone on the block from 24th to 25th Streets is part of the Metropolitan Life's Home Office Building, Waid & Corbett, architects (1931-32). At 42nd Street, dominating the northern end of the vista, stands the huge Pan Am Building, built in 1962. (8/8/75; 10:51.)

West Side of Fourth Avenue, Looking North from East 31st Street (1890)

Fourth Avenue from East 32nd Street north to the Harlem River was officially renamed Park Avenue in 1888. The "merchant king" A. T. Stewart erected the lavish seven-story Park Avenue Hotel in 1876-78, from a design by John Kellum, as a Home for Working Women. Its prices were so high and its regulations so stringent that it soon failed and became a public hotel. It is interesting to note the differences between the costly cast-iron Park Avenue Hotel and its neighbor, the wooden three-story frame Brandes Hotel, a remnant of rural New York. At the extreme right is the entrance to the tunnel built by the New York & Harlem Railroad from 34th to 41st Streets to ease the Murray Hill grade on Park Avenue. This tunnel was originally constructed in an open cut with retaining walls, but was roofed over around 1854. The position of the cart outside the Bridgeport Market seems to indicate that there was no law against parking close to a fire hydrant in 1890.

84

West Side of Park Avenue, Looking North from East 32nd Street (1974)

The west side of Park Avenue presents a fairly solid wall of high modern buildings as far as the eye can see. The Park Avenue Hotel was demolished in 1925. In its place rose the No. 2 Park Avenue office building (center), Ely Jacques Kahn, architect, 1926-27. To the right of it, on 33rd to 34th Streets, stands the former Vanderbilt Hotel, designed by Warren & Wetmore and built in 1910. It was converted into an apartment building in 1965. After the streetcars ceased running through the Park Avenue Tunnel, at the far right, in 1935, it was converted for passenger automobile use and reopened in October 1937. Of all the varied buildings visible in our 1890 photo, not one is standing today. Only the tunnel remains. (9/12/74; 10:10.)

Park Avenue, North to East 42nd Street at Grand Central Station (1887)

In the foreground is the north exit of the Murray Hill Tunnel, with horsecar tracks coming up the ramp and leading into the station at the right or turning into 42nd Street at the left. The tunnel, running through the middle of Park Avenue, was originally built from 34th to 41st Streets, so that steam trains could travel uptown from the terminal at East 27th Street without climbing Murray Hill. After 1859, the tunnel was used exclusively by horsecars, followed by electric cars after 1898. The handsome Victorian station, designed by I. C. Buckhout, was opened October 9, 1871 for the use of the three railroads whose names are written on its three pavilions. The big train shed was built directly behind the station section. Travelers could not only proceed directly to the horsecars in the station, but could go from the Station Annex, on the far right, to the station platform of the spur of the Third Avenue elevated or to the carriages in the street.

Park Avenue, North to East 42nd Street at Grand Central Station (1974)

The original station was extensively remodeled and enlarged in 1898-1900. It was demolished in 1910 for the present Grand Central Station, which was designed in the Beaux-Arts style by Reed & Stem, Warren & Wetmore, and was built 1910-13. Jules-Alexis Coutan's great sculptural group *Transportation* was installed on top of the station in 1914. The station, an architectural landmark, contains one of the few great interior spaces left in New York City. In 1917, a traffic viaduct (left) running around the station was built to bring traffic directly from the southern section of Park Avenue to the continuation of Park Avenue at East 46th Street. The statue of Commodore Vanderbilt, president of the New York Central Railroad from 1868 to 1877, is visible in front of the lower part of the station's large center window. On the left, above the viaduct, is the former Airlines Terminal, built in 1940. The Hotel Biltmore rises behind the Airlines Terminal Building and at the right of the hotel is the top of the 23-story Yale Club Building. The great wall of windows rising behind the station is the Pan American Building, designed by Walter Gropius and erected in 1962. (12/10/74; 1:55.)

Park Avenue, Looking South from East 56th Street (1905)

On May 1, 1834 the New York and Harlem Railroad first carried passengers on upper Fourth Avenue (named Park Avenue in 1888) from 42nd Street to 85th Street in Yorkville. By 1848 the New Haven Railroad entered Manhattan along the Fourth Avenue tracks. Because of increased traffic, smoke and noise, the city eventually required the railroad to lower its tracks into an open cut or tunnel from 46th to 96th Streets. Here we see seven tracks, of which three are temporary, while new tracks are being laid preparatory to electrification. A retaining wall is being built on each side of the cut to allow additional space for an enlarged station approach. In spite of the presence of the railroad, Park Avenue was lined with brownstone and brick residences. Commercial buildings existed one block below the 54th Street bridge crossing (center). On the left, between 53rd and 52nd Streets, stands the five-story Steinway piano factory. The building with the high cupola is the Schaefer Brewery, located between 51st and 50th Streets.

Park Avenue, Looking South from East 56th Street (1975)

Nothing remains of the structures in the 1905 photo save the railroad, now running under the avenue. Starting about 1910, Park Avenue began to change gradually from an avenue of homes and small apartment buildings (mixed with a number of shanties and stables) to a thoroughfare lined with luxury apartment houses for the wealthy. The railroad cut had been covered over around 1880 and a raised mall containing shrubbery enclosed by an iron fence was built in the center of the avenue up to 96th Street. The mall was narrowed and a new iron fence was installed in 1928-29. Below East 59th Street Park Avenue has been undergoing another change from luxury apartments to modern glass-curtain office buildings. In this view all the buildings on Park Avenue on the blocks from 56th to 44th Streets are fairly new high-rise office buildings except for one apartment (the third building on the left), two hotels, a church and a clubhouse. In the center, the New York General Building Tower (formerly New York Central) is silhouetted against the great glass wall of the newer Pan Am Building, built in 1962 on East 45th Street from Vanderbilt Avenue to Depew Place. (12/2/75; 10:05.)

Madison Avenue, North from East 27th Street (1885)

Madison Avenue was developed in the early 1850s as a fine New York residential street, second only to Fifth Avenue. In addition to the many stately homes of the wealthy and a number of outstanding churches, there were several eight- to ten-story elevator apartment houses built along Madison Avenue during the 1880s. Two of these early elevator apartments, both built in 1882, are visible here: one stands at the northwest corner of East 28th Street; the other, an eleven-story apartment (completely modernized in 1962), is on the right, at East 30th Street. The short spire marks the Rutgers Presbyterian Church (1873), which became the Scottish Rite Hall in 1889. It was demolished in 1903. Here is Madison Avenue with carriages and delivery wagons, gas lamps at the corners and ladies wearing bustles.

Madison Avenue, North from East 27th Street (1975)

Madison Avenue presents the familiar canyon of tall office, loft and salesroom buildings. A majority of the buildings shown here were built before or during the 1920s; the major exception is the 18-story annex building of the New York Life Insurance Co. (right) between 27th and 28th Streets, built in 1962. On the left, at the southwest corner of East 29th Street, is the Hotel Seville, built in 1904 on the site of the Scottish Rite Hall. On the 27th Street corner a new concrete trash container displays an advertisement; the space is rented by the city to bring in additional income. (11/4/75; 1:40.)

Madison Avenue, Looking South from East 30th Street (1911)

Although Madison Avenue retains its residential character in this view, commercial inroads can be seen. In the center stands the Metropolitan Life Insurance Building at 23rd Street. Its tower, the final section of the building to be constructed, was the tallest structure in New York from 1909 until 1912. The tower to the left of the Metropolitan's was modeled after the Giralda in Seville. It was designed by Stanford White as part of his Madison Square Garden, which stood on the block bounded by Madison and Fourth Avenues and 26th and 27th Streets. Built in 1890, this second Garden (the first had started life in 1857 as a railway station, later becoming P. T. Barnum's Grand Roman Hippodrome and Gilmore's Garden) was the center of New York sporting events. It presented, among other things, the Horse Show, six-day bicycle races, Buffalo Bill's Wild West Show, prizefights and circuses. It also housed a theater and a restaurant where White was shot to death by Harry Thaw in 1906. Augustus Saint-Gaudens' statue of Diana, which stood atop the tower, was removed when the building was torn down in 1925, and was eventually installed in the Philadelphia Museum of Fine Arts. In the photo we see a fine example of the flagstone sidewalks for which the city was noted.

Madison Avenue, Looking South from East 30th Street (1974)

By 1975 the stretch of Madison Avenue below East 30th Street was built up with high office buildings to just about the economical limit. The New York Life Insurance Building, whose lower three stories show immediately above the bus in the center of the avenue, stands on the site of the old Madison Square Garden. The Metropolitan Tower, on the left, remains at the foot of the avenue. Here the view of it is partially blocked by the recently completed skyscraper at the southeast corner of East 26th Street and Madison Avenue, on the site of the home of Winston Churchill's maternal grandfather, Leonard Jerome. The Hotel Seville (right), at East 29th Street, remains as it was when built in 1904, and, after 71 years, still operates under the same name. The building with the two water tanks, seen at the end of Madison Avenue, is also an old survivor. (9/30/74; 11:15.)

Madison Avenue, Northwest Corner of East 72nd Street (1886)

One of the earliest large New York City mansions was the Charles L. Tiffany residence at 19 East 72nd Street. This immense structure was designed in 1882 by Stanford White of the famous firm of McKim, Mead and White. The residence, constructed in 1883-85 at a cost of over $500,000, was designed as a triple house. The lower floors were for the owner, the founder and senior member of the well-known jewelry house of Tiffany & Co. The third floor was designed for Tiffany's daughter, and the floors within the roof were designed for his son, Louis C. Tiffany, who had White follow his specifications in decorating his apartment in the old Dutch style. White designed the exterior of the Tiffany mansion in the Romanesque style—a reflection of his training with H. H. Richardson, the outstanding proponent of the style.

Madison Avenue, Northwest Corner of East 72nd Street (1975)

In place of the Tiffany mansion (demolished 1936), Rosario Candela and Mott B. Schmidt designed a 17-story luxury apartment building (1937) with two all-stone fronts. This section of Madison Avenue has many fine apartment houses with small elite shops catering to the wealthy customers of the upper East Side. The four-story-and-basement brownstone residence one block north at the northwest corner of East 73rd Street remains, with its lower floors altered for business use. (3/11/75; 12:35.)

West Side of Sixth Avenue, from Greenwich Avenue to West 10th Street (1864)

The original Jefferson Market was established in 1833 at the northwest corner of Sixth and Greenwich Avenues. It consisted of a one-story market building with a sidewalk canopy and a two-story meat market with meeting rooms and a cupola, originally used as a fire watchtower. The eight-story wooden watchtower (center), erected later, was one of the tallest in the city. The open level in the tower contained the bell that sounded fire alarms. Up to West 10th Street,

Sixth Avenue is lined with five two-story residential buildings with stores on the ground floors. The buildings from 10th to 11th Streets are three-story. The horsecar in the photo belongs to the Sixth Avenue line, one of the oldest in the city (established in 1852). It ran downtown to Broadway and Vesey Street. By 1864 Greenwich Village had been firmly settled; "uptown" was developing from 23rd to 34th Streets.

West Side of Sixth Avenue, from Greenwich Avenue to West 10th Street (1926)

The old Jefferson Market complex was replaced by a new one designed by architects Withers and Vaux in 1874. It consisted of the market, a courthouse and a house of detention, all in the Victorian Gothic style. A fire watchtower, with clock, was appended to the courthouse. The tall House of Detention, with a police station, rises directly behind the three-story market building. Although of varying heights, the three buildings blend together in this unusually well-designed civic complex. The Sixth Avenue "el" had been completed and was in operation by 1878. The three-story buildings between 10th and 11th Streets are unchanged.

Lenox Avenue, North from West 124th Street (1901)

Unpaved except for street crossings and the stone blocks alongside the car tracks, tree-lined Lenox Avenue was the second-busiest shopping street in Harlem. The main shopping thoroughfare was 125th Street, where a streetcar of the 125th Street crosstown line is seen at the crossing. In 1895 the car tracks on Lenox Avenue were the first to be electrified in Manhattan. Because overhead wires were prohibited in Manhattan, a slot was used between the rails for electric contact. The hoist-and-rigging setup beyond 125th Street is taking soundings for the future Lenox Avenue-145th Street branch of the West Side I.R.T. subway, which opened on November 23, 1904 with a station at 125th Street. Unusual for Manhattan are two three-story wooden frame buildings with wooden siding—the second building on the left and the one on the right at the northeast corner of 125th Street.

Lenox Avenue, North from West 124th Street (1975)

After the opening of the subway, Lenox Avenue gradually became more commercial. The streetcars are gone, as are the trees and horses. There has been little new construction. Generally, older buildings have been renovated with stores on the ground floors and apartments above. Steel shutters close off the store fronts since this photo was taken on a Sunday. In the distance, around 135th and 140th Streets, several high-rise developments have recently been constructed. Business buildings have replaced the two wooden structures of the 1901 photo. (3/18/75, 11.05.)

Seventh Avenue, Looking South to Greenwich Avenue and West 11th Street (1912)

Until 1913-18, when the Broadway-Seventh Avenue I.R.T. subway was opened below 42nd Street, Seventh Avenue ended at this corner. To facilitate the construction of the subway, the avenue was cut through to join Varick Street at Carmine Street. The new section of the avenue was named Seventh Avenue South. Standing directly in the way of oncoming construction, the Monahan's Express Co. building was demolished in 1913. The building on the left, with the stone quoins at the corner, is St. Vincent's Hospital, built in 1906.

Seventh Avenue at Greenwich Avenue,
Looking South down Seventh Avenue South (1975)

The new extension, although not very attractive, provided a much-needed traffic link with downtown Manhattan. St. Vincent's Hospital remains, but without the former handsome iron fence. With its various additions, it has become one of the great hospitals of New York. The two brick residences across from the hospital on Greenwich Avenue still stand, but two diners and a gas station occupy part of the site of Monahan's Express Co. A large 18-story modern apartment building dominates Seventh Avenue South at Charles Street. In the distance are the 110-story twin towers of the World Trade Center. The two solid-looking loft buildings to the right of center are located on Varick Street, where Seventh Avenue South ends. (11/4/75; 1:10.)

Seventh Avenue, Looking North from West 23rd Street (1914)

Wooden planking covered Seventh Avenue while the I.R.T. Seventh Avenue subway was under construction. On September 23, 1915, a terrific explosion of dynamite turned Seventh Avenue from 23rd to 25th Streets into a 30-foot-deep chasm, burying a streetcar and killing and injuring many persons. The damage was promptly repaired and the subway was completed. Service began at the 23rd Street station on July 1, 1918. The tall Mercantile Building (right) at West 24th Street, designed by Frederick Squires in 1912, was built at the same time that the block-wide building (I. E. Ditmars, architect) across the avenue was being completed for the National Cloak and Suit Co. In the far distance stands the Times Building Tower at Times Square. Traffic was still predominantly horse-drawn and curb parking was readily available. In 1914, there were no traffic lights; traffic was directed by policemen standing in the center of street crossings. The white-clad streetcleaner (left of center) is busy with his broom. The corner saloon provides customers with easy entrance and exit by three entrances with swinging doors as well as by the family entrance on the side.

Seventh Avenue, Looking North from West 23rd Street (1974)

Several of the buildings from 23rd to 26th Streets survive from the 1914 photo with various alterations. The loft building on the northwest corner of 24th Street is now the United States Navy Recruiting and Research Center. The streetcars and their tracks were discontinued in 1936 and the corner saloon has been gone for many years. Traffic is heavy on Seventh Avenue, which offers direct access to Broadway and the upper West Side, the garment center and Penn Station, and to lower Manhattan and the Holland Tunnel. (10/10/74; 11:30.)

Seventh Avenue, North from West 32nd Street (1924)

The classic facade of the entrance to McKim, Mead and White's Pennsylvania Station is visible on the left at West 33rd Street. Built in 1905-10, the station, located between Seventh and Eighth Avenues and between 31st and 33rd Streets, was the largest in the world. Its waiting room was the biggest and one of the finest anywhere. The Pennsylvania Hotel, across the avenue, was the world's largest hotel when built in 1918-19. On billboards at the northwest corner of 33rd Street are signs advertising five-cent cigars, B.V.D.'s and Cecil B. DeMille's moving picture *The Ten Commandments*, which had opened at the George M. Cohan Theatre in December of 1923. Traffic is being directed by a mounted traffic policeman, visible in the center, to the right of the second streetcar. There are three types of lampposts at this part of Seventh Avenue: on the left, a special type for the station; on the right, a single, hanging lamp and just beyond the hotel canopy stands a double-drop lamp, similar to those on Fifth Avenue. Note the early checkered cabs.

Seventh Avenue, North from West 32nd Street (1975)

The demolition of Pennsylvania Station in 1963-66 was a great architectural loss to New York City and the country. The Bowery Savings Bank has rebuilt the west side of the avenue from 33rd to 34th Streets. The former Pennsylvania Hotel is now the Statler Hilton. The garment center from 34th to 40th Streets is solidly built up with office and loft buildings. In 1930, the 48-story Nelson Tower was built at the northwest corner of 34th Street. The year before, the 44-story Navarre Building (the tall tower building behind the Nelson) had been erected on the site of the Navarre Hotel at 38th Street. In the distance the top of the Paramount Building clock tower is visible at Times Square (4/17/75; 2:10.)

Northwest Corner of Eighth Avenue and West 23rd Street (1933)

At this time the Grand Opera House was the oldest theater in continuous operation in New York. The imposing building opened on January 9, 1868 as Pike's Opera House. It boasted a marble exterior, the largest foyer of any theater in the city, an 80-foot stage with a depth of 70 feet and a seating capacity of 3500. It was bought by Jim Fisk and Jay Gould in 1869 and was renamed the Grand Opera House. Operas, spectacles and dramatic productions were presented there and Fisk's funeral was held in his offices in the building in 1872. After a period of presenting vaudeville, followed by mixed bills of motion pictures and vaudeville, the theater became a movie house until the 92-year-old building was destroyed by fire in 1960. The Cornish Arms Hotel, adjacent to the Grand Opera House, was erected in 1926 as a first-class hotel for the Chelsea district. Shoeshine boys have set up shop at the entrance to the IND. subway and in front of the corner dress shop.

Northwest Corner of Eighth Avenue and West 23rd Street (1974)

The Carver Federal Savings & Loan Association built a branch building on the site of the Opera House in 1963. The large metal cornice across the top front of the Cornish Arms Hotel roof was recently removed because it was a safety hazard. In 1962 the International Ladies Garment Workers Union developed the section from Eighth to Ninth Avenues and from 24th to 29th Streets into a high-rise apartment group called Penn Station South Houses, which provides reasonably priced living quarters for the union's members, convenient to the garment district where they work. (10/10/74; 11:00.)

Eighth Avenue, North from West 111th Street (1893)

The opening of the Eighth Avenue "el" by the Manhattan Railway Co. on September 17, 1879 provided the area from 110th to 155th Streets with quick transportation to South Ferry. For years following the opening, especially between 1890 and 1905, Harlem was built up with five-story apartment buildings with ground-floor stores on the avenues and with three- and four-story private residences on the side streets. This view shows one of the highest sections of the "el" at the point where it came out of an S-curve from Columbus Avenue at 110th Street. The tracks of the Eighth Avenue horsecar line can be seen in the muddy, unpaved avenue below. It carried its passengers all the way to Broadway and Vesey Street. The five-story apartment near the southeast corner of West 112th Street is nearing completion and a similar building is under construction on the west side of the avenue at 114th Street.

112

Eighth Avenue, North from West 111th Street (1975)

The "el" was torn down in 1940, eliminating filth and noise and providing more light and air. The streetcar tracks are also gone. The IND. subway, running under Eighth Avenue, has provided transportation to all parts of the city since it was completed in 1932. The five-story apartment house, under construction in the 1893 photo, remains with little change. There has been little progress toward renovation or new building up to 155th Street. (3/18/75; 11:50.)

Lower Manhattan, Looking South from the Brooklyn Bridge (1886)

The construction of the Brooklyn Bridge (dedicated 1883) made possible panoramic views of lower Manhattan such as this one, taken in the same year in which the Statue of Liberty (barely visible on the horizon, left of center) had been unveiled. The photographer took this photo from the bridge's pedestrian walk. From left to right we see Governors Island, the Upper Bay, the East River and Manhattan with its ships lining the South Street piers and its many low, steep-roofed loft buildings. The eye finally rests on the two tallest structures in Manhattan: the tower of G. B. Post's Produce Exchange (completed 1885), in the center of the photo, and the spire of Richard Upjohn's Trinity Church on the right. Steamboats, ferryboats, tugs and sailing ships comprised the principal harbor traffic at this time. A ferryboat is seen approaching the Fulton Ferry slip on South Street.

Lower Manhattan, Looking South from the Brooklyn Bridge (1974)

Except for some reinforcements, road changes, and the elimination of trolleys and "el" cars, the Brooklyn Bridge remains the same. The ships' masts are gone and a modern highway runs over South Street. The greatest change has been the growth of skyscrapers in the financial district, the newer box-like forms contrasting with the older tapered tower buildings. Only one large building, at the foot of Wall Street (No. 120), represents the stepped style popular in the 1920s and early 1930s. The five tallest buildings visible here are, left to right: The Chemical Bank at 55 Water Street (1972); the First National City Trust Co. at 20 Exchange Place, the tallest stone building in the downtown area when it was built in 1931; the 60 Wall Tower (1932; tallest in this group); the 40 Wall Tower (1930) and finally the Chase-Manhattan Building (1960) at Nassau and Liberty Streets. (12/11/74; 10:50.)

Lower East Side, North from the Brooklyn Bridge (1885)

Looking north from the Manhattan tower of the Brooklyn Bridge, we see the congested lower East Side with the piers and ferry slips alongside South Street, from James Slip to beyond Market Slip (extreme right). Directly below the bridge is the steam-powered ferryboat *Alaska*, used by the James Street Ferry to carry passengers up the East River to Long Island City in Queens County. At Pier 32, the Long Island Railroad, with four carfloats filled with freight boxcars, had its freight depot. The old Clyde Line was located to the right at Pier 33. Further along, opposite the two-story Catherine Market building, to the right, across South Street, is the Catherine Street Ferryhouse, where people took the ferry to Main Street in downtown Brooklyn. At the lower right, one can see the bridge roadway cable reinforcement attached to the stone tower with an iron pin. Beyond the waterfront is the great mass of walk-up, cold-water tenement buildings which made up most of the East Side, where many European immigrants settled.

Lower East Side, North from the Brooklyn Bridge (1974)

Not only are the ferry slips and the piers gone, but South Street now lies under the Franklin D. Roosevelt elevated highway. The Manhattan Bridge (upper right) was completed in 1909, making a third connection by bridge between Brooklyn and Manhattan. Most of the older tenement buildings have been cleared away and replaced by new schools and various modern high-rise housing groups. On the left are the Alfred E. Smith Houses. The Knickerbocker Village houses are in the center. Beyond the Manhattan Bridge are the Rutgers Houses and LaGuardia Houses. In 1927 William Randolph Hearst built the six-story white building on South Street (center) for producing his newspaper *The New York Evening Journal*. It is now the headquarters of the *New York Post*. One thing that has not changed through the years is the Brooklyn Bridge roadway reinforcement cable, with the attachment to the stone tower. (12/11/74; 10:40.)

State Street, Looking North from the Northwest Corner of Whitehall Street (1908)

At one time, State Street was a fine residential street, with Federal row residences facing Battery Park. Four of these, built in 1793 (Nos. 1, 2, 3, 6), can be seen. (No. 7, still extant in 1908, is not visible.) The corner building, No. 1, built for John Coles, a well-known merchant, has the double chimney and the three curved windows (in the fourth-floor gable on the Whitehall Street side) characteristic of the early Federal style. The Seamen's Church Institute occupied No. 1 from 1902 to 1913. For many years the British Consulate had an office for seamen in No. 2. Nos. 1, 2 and 3 were torn down in 1913 to make way for the 12-story South Ferry Office Building. The six-story building at No. 4, occupied by the German Lutheran Immigration House, was demolished in 1913, along with the four-story loft building at No. 5, and was replaced by a six-story office building. No. 6, partly visible at the extreme left and one of the original Federal residences, was used for many years by the Leo House for German Immigrants. This organization added an additional story, with a new cornice, during its occupancy. Part of the rear of the United States Customs House appears at the far right. Designed by Cass Gilbert (architect of the Woolworth Building), it was built in 1901-07.

State Street, Looking North from the Northwest Corner of Whitehall Street (1975)

The 33-story office building that dominates the corner of State and Whitehall Streets has three names—The Schroder Building, 44 Whitehall Street and No. 1 State Street Plaza. In order to avoid setbacks and build higher structures, architects of new buildings now usually leave a portion of land in front or on the sides as a breathing space for the public. The space, called a plaza, becomes part of the address. The 36-story skyscraper directly behind, at the right (called No. 1 Battery Park Plaza or 24 Whitehall Street), was built in 1969-70 and has another plaza. The former Customs House is at the far right. The only historic building remaining on State Street is the last of the 1793 houses, No. 7, now used as the rectory of the Shrine of Saint Elizabeth Seton. Only the east portion is visible at the far left. The west portion, built in 1806, has a curved porch designed by John McComb, Jr., one of the architects of New York's City Hall. (6/11/75; 1:15.)

Broad Street, North from Water Street (1909)

In New Amsterdam a canal, the Heere Gracht, ran down the middle of what is now Broad Street from the waterfront to about the site of Exchange Place. When the canal was filled in in 1676, its spacious width gave the street its present name. This part of Broad Street is located at the lower edge of the downtown financial district. In this photo many older buildings can be seen, but larger office buildings were making inroads from the Stock Exchange section of Broad Street to its end at South Street. The substantial-looking seven-story office building in the right center was built in 1890 as one of the early telephone buildings. It was torn down recently; its site is now used for one of the ugly parking lots that mar today's urban landscape. The third building on the right is the famous Fraunces Tavern. It was built in 1719 as a private residence for Etienne De Lancey. It became a tavern (the Queen's Head, owned by Samuel Fraunces) and was raised two stories in 1763. It was used as headquarters of the Chamber of Commerce, among other activities. On its second floor General Washington said farewell to his officers on December 4, 1783. The tavern was bought in dilapidated condition by the Sons of the Revolution in 1904. Completely reconstructed as a colonial tavern in 1907, it is a popular dining place. The open horsecar of the Central Park, North and East River Railroad is turning into Water Street to continue its route up to 59th Street.

Broad Street, North from Water Street (1974)

Here we see the result of the growth of lower Broad Street into a modern skyscraper canyon. On the right, the block from Water to Pearl Streets has the only remaining older building. The five-story building at the northeast corner of Broad and Water Streets has changed little in 95 years. The fire escape has been relocated, the wooden shutters are gone and the principal occupant is a now-rare corner grocery store. The adjoining three-story building, on the left, was renovated, two stories being removed, and has become an annex to Fraunces Tavern, adjacent on the left. The Anglers Club has been a tenant on the second floor since 1940; the third floor is used as a Colonial museum. The 35-story building with the arched entrance at 50 William Street is the International Telephone & Telegraph Building. The first three buildings on the west side of Broad Street (left) are, from Water Street: No. 104 (New York Telephone); No. 90 (Stone & Webster); No. 80 (Maritime Exchange). The tall 48-story building at the bend of Broad Street (center) is No. 30 Broad Street Building, built in 1931-32 for the Continental Bank. (12/3/74; 1:10.)

Broad Street, North from Pearl Street (1882)

Broad Street was paved with cobblestones, was lighted by gas and was crisscrossed with telephone and telegraph wires. A saloon stood at the corner. New office buildings had not yet intruded into the lower Broad Street area. Stores flourished in the older buildings, some of which had been built with the steep roofs of the early 1800s. Fraunces Tavern stands on the right, at Pearl and Broad Streets, with the sign "Washington's Headquarters." At this time the building was in rundown condition.

Broad Street, North from Pearl Street (1974)

Broad Street is now paved with smooth asphalt and is lighted by electricity. Wiring is underground and the corner saloon is gone. Only a few of the shepherd's-crook type of streetlight (right) remain in the city. Most have been replaced by the newer models, similar to the one across the street. Two parking lots extend from Pearl to South William Streets. They were created by the demolition of two older office buildings—the Telephone Building of 1890 and the All America Cables Building of 1919. Beyond stands the 35-story International Telephone & Telegraph Building. It was erected in two sections: one running along Broad to Beaver Street (1927), the other running from Broad along South William Street (1930). (12/11/74; 1:10.)

Coenties Slip, Looking Northwest from Front Street toward Pearl Street (1904)

The Third Avenue elevated line was originally intended as an extension of the Ninth Avenue elevated line from South Ferry, running up the East Side to Harlem. On August 26, 1878, the Third Avenue "el" was opened from South Ferry to Grand Central Station at 42nd Street. The route made it necessary to construct a sharp S-curve in order to turn left from Front Street, cross Coenties Slip, then turn right into Pearl Street to proceed uptown. The elevated trains were forced to move slowly over the curve, thereby providing the passengers with exciting views of the South Street waterfront and lower Manhattan. The cluster of tall office buildings which form a backdrop for this scene are centered around the principal streets of the downtown financial district— Broadway, Broad, Wall and William Streets. The 20-story building with rear sections visible on the left is the south part of the Broad-Exchange Building, the largest office building in the city from 1901 to 1906. The light stone office building with the dark cornice (left center) is the recently completed 20-story Corn Exchange Bank Building on William Street. The building with the high mansard roof, conical tower and flag flying, is the 1885 Cotton Exchange Building, designed by George B. Post, at the southeast corner of William and Beaver Streets. Facing the "el" are several of the older four- and five-story residential and loft buildings.

Looking Northwest from Jeanette Park toward Coenties Slip (1975)

Few locations in Manhattan show greater change than the Coenties Slip area. This view looks across Jeanette Park toward Water Street and beyond, where Coenties Slip runs from Water to Pearl Street. Two of the older five-story buildings remain on Pearl Street facing the Slip, at right center. Two other older buildings shown in the 1904 photo stand behind the tree on the right, facing the east side of Water Street. The "el" was demolished in 1951. The section of Front Street that ran through this area no longer exists. In its place stand two skyscrapers on each side of Jeanette Park—Nos. 2 and 4 New York Plaza (left) and 55 Water Street (right). None of the tall office buildings visible in the center of the photo was built before 1927. The building in the center, with the crown-like top, is the International Telephone Building on Broad Street. Jeanette Park has been entirely renovated and enlarged, with a sunken pit and decorative water, uncomfortable backless round benches and sparse foliage. To quote Ada Louise Huxtable, "It has no sense of history or humanity." (8/8/75; 1:15.)

(1887)

(1930)

128

(1975)

Centre Street, West Side, North from Leonard Street

(1887)

The Collect Pond, a placid body of water where the public enjoyed boating and fishing in summer and ice skating in winter, was located in the area around Centre and Leonard Streets. As New York advanced northward, the pond became an obstruction; in 1817 it was filled in. A House of Detention and Criminal Court building was erected on the site of the old pond in 1838-40. Because of its resemblance to an Egyptian tomb, the court and jail buildings were popularly called "the Tombs." A "Bridge of Sighs" was erected across Franklin Street to connect the Tombs with the new Centre Street Criminal Court building in 1894. The Tombs was considered one of the finest examples of neo-Egyptian architecture in the country. Howe and Hummel, a noted law firm, had offices on the first floor of the three-story building at the southwest corner of Leonard Street. A stone carriage block stands at the curb in front of their offices. There is a fine example of a public street clock, placed on the sidewalk by businesses for advertising purposes.

(1930)

The original Tombs was demolished in 1896 and a new and enlarged city prison was built on the site in 1897-1902. This building was larger, with 324 cells, but cold and forbidding in appearance; therefore, it was only natural that the name "the Tombs" be continued. On the next block north, from Franklin to White Streets, New York City built a seven-story Criminal Courts Building (1890-95). The same old "Bridge of Sighs" was re-erected over Franklin Street to connect the new Tombs with its neighbor. A section of this bridge is visible in the center of the photo. In 1929 the heavy classical entrance portico was removed from the front of the Criminal Courts Building. This fine view of the two buildings was made possible by the demolition of all the older structures on the east side of Centre Street, preparatory to the construction of the present huge Criminal Courts Building in 1940. The large L-shaped 17-story loft and office building (1914) rising up in the center of the photo is the 80 Lafayette Street Building, with a section facing Franklin Street.

(1975)

The second Tombs building was torn down in 1947 and in its place the city has recently constructed a small park and a parking lot. Five large courthouses are now grouped around Centre Street. On the left is the edge of the City Health, Hospitals and Sanitation Building (1934-35). Across the park stands the Civil Court Building (1960). The edge of the new (1972-75) Family Court Building is visible, second from the left, facing Lafayette Street. Both the seven-story office building at the northwest corner of Lafayette and Franklin Streets and the 17-story loft and office structure that is built around it have changed very little. (5/15/75; 11:55.)

Chatham Square, Northeast toward the Bowery (1900)

Chatham Square is at the north end of Park Row (formerly Chatham Street). The following streets converge here (clockwise): Mott Street, The Bowery, Division Street and East Broadway (at the corner with the pawnbroker's shop). This was part of the original High Road, the principal highway out of New York City in the early 1700s, which began at Broadway, then ran through Chatham Street and the Square to The Bowery and thence to Boston. In 1878 the Third Avenue elevated was erected through The Bowery on its way to South Ferry, with a branch in Chatham Square to City Hall. In 1880 the Second Avenue elevated line was built through Division Street to Chatham Square, forming a junction with the Third Avenue line and continuing on to South Ferry or City Hall. Here we see a Third Avenue train, consisting of a steam locomotive and five coaches, crossing to the uptown Third Avenue track. New York's Chinatown had its nucleus in and around Mott Street. The various commercial buildings that surround Chatham Square were all built between 1865 and 1875. However, a new building is being started in the middle of the block, on the left, between Mott Street and The Bowery.

Chatham Square, Northeast toward the Bowery (1974)

The last train ran on the Third Avenue "el" on May 12, 1955. The structure was torn down soon after, making Chatham Square a much more open area. Six of the older buildings still stand on the left-hand block from Mott Street to The Bowery. In the middle of this block is the eight-story loft building on which construction had started in the 1900 photo. On the block in the center, between Division Street and East Broadway, one building is gone and another has had its face lifted. The ten-story loft building is still in use. New York's Chinatown now practically surrounds the square, as evidenced by many signs in Chinese. The high-rise apartment, being built by the New York City Housing Administration, is known as Confucius Plaza. (12/6/74; 2:12.)

The Bowery, North from Canal Street (1888)

"The Bowery! The Bowery! I'll never go there any more," ran the popular song about The Bowery when the name stood for the worst vices of a big city. In pre-Colonial days The Bowery was a country lane, running between the "bouweries" (farms) of the Dutch burghers. In the nineteenth century The Bowery developed into the entertainment center of the city, then declined into a notorious avenue, commonly called Skid Row, with mission houses and flophouses. The addition of the Third Avenue elevated in 1878 did nothing to improve the street's appearance. Eventually The Bowery, with the aid of various reform movements, achieved a better reputation and became a street with banks, loft and business buildings plus the inevitable hotels and pawnbroker shops. Here we see the steam-powered elevated trains and several types of horsecars of the Third Avenue line and a single horsecar of the Canal and Grand Street Ferry line about to cross The Bowery. Originally the "el" consisted of a single track on each side of the street, over the sidewalk, as shown here. In 1915 the structure and stations were rebuilt, with the addition of an express track, and were moved to the center of the street, providing more light for pedestrians and stores.

The Bowery, North from Canal Street (1975)

With the streetcars and elevated structure removed, The Bowery became a fine wide avenue for two-way automobile and bus traffic. The two buildings at the extreme right had their fronts rebuilt on a 30-degree angle in order to provide more space for the exit of the Manhattan Bridge, opened in 1909. Many of the older buildings remain and are still in use as loft buildings or cheap hotels. Two of the painted signs on the side buildings seen in the 1888 photo are still visible: "John P. Jube & Co., Carriage Materials" and, farther along The Bowery, "Coogan." At the end of the first block on the right is a modern Chinese theater at the southeast corner of Hester Street. On the left, at the corner of Canal Street, is a Chinese newsstand. (The heart of New York's Chinatown begins directly across Canal Street to the south.) The photo shows the latest type of one-man police car (left). (4/17/75; 2:15.)

Mulberry Street, Looking North toward Canal Street (1900)

Teeming Mulberry Street was the center of the Italian section of the lower East Side—"Little Italy." It was separated from the Jewish quarter by The Bowery, while the adjoining Chinatown district, to the east, was largely confined to Mott, Pell and Doyers Streets. Mulberry Street started near the "Five Points," an intersection of five streets notorious for its general depravity. The Five Points section was eliminated in 1896 and Columbus Park was created on the west side of Mulberry Street where the street bends 30 degrees to the north. This photo, taken less than a block north of the famous Mulberry Bend, shows numerous pushcarts, wagons and tenements. Fire escapes were used for the storage of household goods and for clothes drying; on hot nights people slept on them. Most of the Italians in the area came from southern Italy and Sicily, making Little Italy a colorful, lively and very noisy locality.

Mulberry Street, Looking North toward Canal Street (1975)

Today lower Mulberry Street is still a nominal part of Little Italy, but most of the sidewalk crowd and store owners are Chinese as a result of the growth of Chinatown. Many of the descendants of the earlier Italian immigrants have moved north to Greenwich Village, Brooklyn or Queens, but a large group still lives around Mulberry Street. Every September the big and joyful Italian Festival of San Gennaro, patron saint of Naples, attracts crowds to Mulberry Street. A large number of the older tenement buildings are standing today. The light-brick, three-story building on the right, formerly residential, became a movie theater and then a modern supermarket. The large six-story loft building in the center at the southeast corner of Canal Street has changed very little except for the removal of the fifth-floor cornice. (12/7/75; 1:35.)

Hester Street, West from Essex Street (1904)

The largest and most famous of the foreign settlements in New York was the lower East Side, occupied by great numbers of immigrants from Poland, Russia and Italy. Hester Street was the heart of this vast slum, filled with ugly tenements and littered streets. Pushcarts lined the blocks from end to end, displaying a great variety of goods at low prices. Weather permitting, the street was crowded with people at all hours, the outdoors being more attractive than the cold-water railroad flats. The language of Hester Street was Yiddish and the derby was the popular hat. Several "old-clothes" men stand in the foreground at the left. The line of tenements and small frame buildings is broken only by Public School No. 42 at the northwest corner of Ludlow Street. The ever-present corner saloon provided about the only social life. One could purchase laces, silks, satins and velvets for one price at the trimming store on the left.

Hester Street, West from Essex Street (1975)

Hester Street has a somewhat different look today. Public School No. 42 remains, its heavy cornice removed, but many of the tenements have either been demolished or boarded up. The pushcarts were outlawed in 1940. The corner saloon is gone, but various retail stores sell items such as pickles, religious articles, dried fruits, nuts and spices. Vacant lots appear throughout the lower East Side where an owner has elected to demolish a building rather than modernize it. A great many of the former East Side Jewish and Italian families have relocated, but many others live close to the old neighborhood in the numerous modern high-rise apartment developments that have been built on the lower East Side in recent years. (12/7/75; 2:10.)

Delancey Street, East toward Suffolk Street (1919)

Delancey Street, named after a New York family prominent during the Colonial period, eventually became a principal thoroughfare of the lower East Side, particularly after it was selected as the approach to the Williamsburg Bridge, the world's largest suspension bridge when it was opened by Mayor Seth Low on December 19, 1903. It was necessary to cut through a five-block extension of Delancey Street, called Kenmare Street, from The Bowery to Lafayette Street. In addition, Delancey Street was widened on the south side in order to accommodate the bridge approach and entrance, heavy traffic and four subway entrances. The north side of Delancey Street in this view shows the typical East Side tenements with stores. The buildings on the south side were all put up after the street widening of 1900. In the far center, the large building with the cluster of smokestacks is the American Sugar Refining Company plant, across the East River on the Brooklyn shore. Many people are using the bridge's pedestrian walk.

Delancey Street, East toward Suffolk Street (1975)

Delancey Street now has two names—the entire street from The Bowery to the East River Drive is still Delancey Street, but the center section of the bridge approach, from The Bowery to Clinton Street, has been named Jacob Schiff Parkway. Delancey Street and Jacob Schiff Parkway has become a wide and unobstructed boulevard. Many of the tenements have been demolished on the north side of Delancey Street. The second block, on the left, from Clinton to Attorney Streets, remains almost intact with six of the original eight buildings still standing. Three modern high-rise apartment developments are visible to the left of the bridge approach, bordered by Delancey Street: the Samuel Gompers Houses, Masaryk Towers and finally, closest to the East River Drive, Baruch Houses. The bridge's former footwalk has been converted for vehicular traffic. (6/11/75; 2.15.)

Battery Place from West Street to Broadway (1900)

The shadow on the plaza in the foreground is cast by the headquarters of the New York City Department of Docks at Pier A, where notables arriving by boat were greeted. The steps at the right lead to a basin for sheltering small boats. Rising above the Battery Place Station (center) of the Sixth and Ninth Avenue elevated lines is the Washington Building, at No. 1 Broadway, occupying one of the best locations in New York, with a fine view of the Upper Bay and Hudson River. It was built in 1882-84 by Cyrus W. Field, who laid the first ocean cable, and was the largest office building in America. An additional three stories, plus a three-story cupola, were added in 1885, making the building both the largest and tallest structure in the country until 1890. Opposite, at No. 2 Broadway, is the Produce Exchange Building (1881-84) with its square tower. The 16-story white-brick Bowling Green Building, directly behind No. 1 Broadway, was built by British interests in 1897. It was said to have been largely financed by Queen Victoria. To the left of the 13-story Columbia Building (1890) with the three-story mansard roof rises the tall cupola of the 17-story Manhattan Life Building, the tallest building in New York from 1893-97. At the extreme left is the American Surety Building (1894), at Broadway and the southeast corner of Pine Street, which housed the United States Weather Bureau on its roof.

Barclay Street, Looking West toward Church Street (1975)

St. Peter's Church remains one of the outstanding Greek Revival buildings in the city. The adjoining five-story rectory is also little changed. In 1962 the church was designated a New York City Landmark. The Sixth Avenue "el" is gone, as well as the horsecar tracks and the Belgian-block paving, but there are street lights where there were none before, as well as the inevitable parking meters. The big stone building with the carved eagle at the sixth-floor corner is the Federal Office Building and downtown Post Office, known as 90 Church Street. It was the New York Naval Headquarters during World War II and until 1972. The tall building with the setbacks at the end of Barclay Street is the Manhattan and Queens headquarters of the New York Telephone Co., built in 1924-25. This was one of the first large buildings to be affected by the New York zoning law of the 1920s, which made setbacks mandatory when a building exceeded a certain height. (12/7/75; 11:20.)

Varick Street, West Side from West Houston to Clarkson Streets (1921)

Varick Street was one of the few wide avenues in the Greenwich Village area that held on to many of the buildings dating from the period of 1820-40. The Federal style of house seen in these eight dwellings was very popular in New York. It usually consisted of a cellar, two stories and attic with a sloping roof and one or two dormer windows. The group shown here was built without any embellishments, with plain doorways, cornices and simple lintels over the window openings. The first house, at the northwest corner of West Houston Street, has a clapboard siding. Three of the houses have been altered into stores; all have had their window shutters removed and the glass in the windows of the first two stories has been changed from the typical twelve panes to two. This entire group of buildings was destroyed in 1924. The horsecar tracks shown here are those of the Sixth Avenue ferry line, which ran from the Desbrosses Street Ferry via Varick and Carmine Streets to Sixth Avenue. The line was abandoned in 1919, after using storage-battery cars for six years. On the extreme left is the entrance to the I.R.T. Broadway-Seventh Avenue line subway, opened beneath Varick Street on July 1, 1918. The wreaths hanging in some of the windows indicate that this photo was taken during the Christmas holiday. A horse-drawn van is making a delivery of Horton's ice cream to the corner cigar store.

Varick Street, West Side from West Houston to Clarkson Streets (1974)

The 12-story loft and factory building, No. 225 Varick Street, was built in 1926 to take the place of the former ten dwellings. The four-story building on the right, at Clarkson Street, is a New York City pool and gymnasium building. Built around 1908 as a public bath, it was modernized in 1939. Varick Street, its car tracks and stone blocks covered with asphalt, has become a busy truck thoroughfare because it is a main street to the Holland and Brooklyn Battery Tunnels. (12/11/74; 12:10.)

East Side of Hudson Street, North from Barrow Street (1925)

Hudson Street, a busy commercial traffic thoroughfare on the western edge of Greenwich Village, connects with Eighth Avenue, giving access to upper Manhattan. The tracks used by electric cars on the Eighth Avenue line are visible in the street. In the center section of the east block, from Barrow to Grove Streets, there appear to be five Federal houses, of which only the far house has the typical three second-floor windows and two dormer windows in the roof. The first four houses are really eight dwellings, each only twelve feet eight inches wide. Each one has a store and separate entrance to the second floor, two windows on the second floor and one dormer in the roof. The signs in the corner loft building and the adjoining four Federal houses indicate they are all being vacated for demolition. The handsome five-story building with Mansard roof and tall flagpole is Public School No. 3, built in 1906 at the northeast corner of Grove Street. (The school building of 1818 was replaced by a fairly large four-story school in 1860, which was destroyed by fire in 1905.) Horse-drawn vehicles are still an integral part of transportation in 1925.

146

East Side of Hudson Street, North from Barrow Street (1975)

The Hudson Street block from Barrow to Grove Streets has been completely rebuilt. It now has two six-story apartment buildings, the first-built being the one on the Barrow Street half of the block (1926). Public School No. 3 has remained the same except for the removal of the roof flagpole and balustrade. The planting of trees has given Hudson Street a more attractive and residential appearance. Barrow Street is paved with the same Belgian blocks, but Hudson Street was repaved in 1972. The same light and heavy fire hydrants, side by side at the east corner, are still there. (1/8/75; 12:05.)

Bleecker Street, Northeast Corner of Christopher Street (1925)

Here is a typical Greenwich Village scene—older three-story buildings with stores alongside five- and six-story walk-up tenements such as the Gessner buildings (1872) on the right. The corner building, 329 Bleecker Street, was built between 1802 and 1810. According to legend, the famous grid plan which determined the growth of New York City was drawn up in this very building in 1807-09 before being published in 1811. Actually, the grid-plan building stood next to this one, and was demolished when Bleecker Street was widened in 1828. The south front of 329 Bleecker retains its original wooden clapboards, along with the old storefront, shutters and small attic windows. The western brick wall, with its star-shaped tierod heads, was erected when a section of the building was shorn away in the widening of 1828. The two quarter-round windows and the central round-headed one of the third floor, in what originally may have been a wooden gable end, are features of the Federal style. On the corner, note the old-style lamppost with the unusually high base.

Bleecker Street, Northeast Corner of Christopher Street (1975)

This is one corner that has changed very little in over 100 years. It will stay this way, for the Landmarks Preservation Commission has designated this section of Greenwich Village a historic district. But while the buildings remain the same, the nature of the neighborhood has changed from lower middle class to one attracting younger single people. All the structures in the older photo remain, with only superficial alterations, such as modernized storefronts and new fire escapes required by law. On its southern facade, the corner building has been stuccoed, one gutter has been removed and the third-floor windows have been enlarged. On the west side, the front has been modernized and the new fire escape substitutes a stair for the old ladder type. The attractive star-shaped tierod heads have been changed to square heads. (5/6/75; 3:05.)

Bleecker Street, West from Broadway toward Mercer Street (1917)

New York City incorporated the world's first street railway, the New York and Harlem Railroad Co., on April 25, 1831. On November 14, 1832, New York started operation of the world's first horsecar, which ran through The Bowery from Prince to 14th Streets. Because they were such an improvement over the omnibus, a large network of horsecar lines was gradually developed in Manhattan. By 1874, it reached almost every section of the city. Cable and electric cars gradually replaced the horsecars, which finally ceased running after 85 years of service in Manhattan. Here the old No. 97 poses on Bleecker Street near Broadway, having just made the last horsecar run in the city on July 26, 1917.

Bleecker Street, West from Broadway toward Mercer Street (1975)

Bleecker Street has lost its horsecars, but the street has become a crosstown thoroughfare from The Bowery to Abingdon Square at Eighth Avenue, while the section from West Broadway to Sixth Avenue has become the center of much of Greenwich Village's nightlife. The six-story former loft building at the northeast corner of Mercer Street (center) remains. Entirely renovated in 1971, it is now the headquarters of the National Puerto Rican Forum. Beyond Mercer Street stands one of the two 17-story, three-block-long buildings of the Washington Square Village Housing Development, erected in 1958. Two familiar sights of New York City appear here—the excavation in the street and the convenient frankfurter cart. (5/15/75; 3:20.)

East 14th Street, West from Third Avenue toward Irving Place (1893)

By 1893 New York's entertainment world had moved up to the Herald Square area, but East 14th Street, once the city's operatic, musical and theatrical center, still maintained a score of attractions. Occupying the west wing of the imposing four-story Tammany Hall (right) is Tony Pastor's vaudeville theater. The Tammany Society, founded in 1789 as a benevolent group, became a powerful political "machine" of the Democratic Party. Its corruption under the rule of "Boss" Tweed is infamous. The Academy of Music, next door, opened in 1854 as an opera house. It was burned out in 1866, but was rebuilt and continued presenting opera until 1887, when it lost out to the competition being offered by the newer Metropolitan Opera, and became a dramatic house. The immensely popular rural play *The Old Homestead* played there for three years. In this photo it is featuring one of David Belasco's greatest hits, *The Girl I Left Behind Me*. The small five-story Irving Place Hotel occupies the northwest corner at Irving Place. The four-story building, located in the middle of the next block, with a pillared portico and a tall flagpole on the roof, is Steinway Hall. For over 25 years it was the classical music center of the country, and the headquarters for Steinway pianos.

East 14th Street, West from Third Avenue toward Irving Place (1974)

Occupying almost the entire block from Third Avenue to Irving Place, from East 14th to East 15th Streets, is the Consolidated Edison Headquarters Building, formerly the Consolidated Gas Co., before its merger with the New York Edison Co. The immense building, with its 30-story clock tower, was built in four sections between 1911 and 1929. It remains incomplete; the final section of the building is to rise on Third Avenue where the company now maintains its own parking lot. On the northwest corner of Irving Place, the Irving Hotel remains as a furnished rooming house. Steinway Hall has been replaced by a six-story loft building. Except for a new two-story building built as an Automat restaurant, the other buildings on this block remain, all with various alterations. (12/11/74; 9:50.)

Union Square, South End at Fourth Avenue and East 14th Street, Looking West (1893)

Extending from 14th to 17th Streets and from Broadway to Fourth Avenue, Union Square has been a public park since 1809. Like Speaker's Corner in London's Hyde Park, it has long been a mecca for soapbox orators. This photo was probably taken on an early Sunday morning, for on 14th Street—a popular and important shopping center—stores are closed, there is little traffic, and only a few pedestrians are evident. The splendid equestrian statue of George Washington (1856), by Henry K. Brown, stands at the right. The square contains Bartholdi's statue of Lafayette (1876), visible to the left of Washington, as well as Brown's statue of Lincoln (not visible). The ornate structure on the far left, at the southwest corner of Broadway and 14th Street, is the Domestic Sewing Machine Building, tallest in New York when built in 1872-73. In the center of the photo stands the nine-story Lincoln Building (1885), R. H. Robertson, architect. Adjoining, to the right, is the Spingler Building, burned out by a fire. The building had been erected in 1872 on the site of the old Spingler House, where board and lodging could be had for $3.50 a day. The cast-iron building (far right), designed by John Kellum in 1869, was occupied by Tiffany's Jewelry House from 1870 until 1905. 14th Street is lined with shops, but in the distance, on the south side, is the spire of the Annunciation Episcopal Church.

*Union Square, South End at Fourth Avenue and East 14th Street,
Looking West (1974)*

The southern section of Union Square is a mixture of the old and the new in architecture. When the Square was replanned and entirely done over in 1928-32, the Washington and Lincoln statues were relocated in the new central mall; the Lafayette statue was placed near the west entrance at 15th Street. 14th Street continues to be a popular shopping center. May's has built a new modern store building and has expanded into the adjoining office building, which replaced the former Domestic Sewing Machine Building in 1927. On the right, facing the square, the recently cleaned Lincoln Building remains. The eight-story Spingler Building next door, built in 1896, replaced the original Spingler Building. In the left center, on the southwest corner of 14th Street and Fifth Avenue, stands the 16-story former Van Schaick loft and office building, built in 1907-08. A modern high rise apartment house is seen behind the Lincoln Building. (10/2/74; 11:30.)

West 23rd Street, Looking East toward Sixth Avenue (1874)

Vine-covered homes and shade trees marked 23rd Street over a century ago. It was not until 1878 that the Sixth Avenue elevated railroad was erected, but the 23rd Street Crosstown horsecar line was already a year old. 23rd Street did not become commercial for another ten years. The handsome Victorian building at the northeast corner of Sixth Avenue and 23rd Street is the Masonic Temple, headquarters of the Masonic Order in New York, where over 90 lodges met regularly. Designed by Napoleon Le Brun, it was built in 1870-72. Sixteen years later, Le Brun designed the Metropolitan Life Insurance Building, built only a block and a half east at 23rd Street and Madison Avenue. The six-story building beyond the brownstone residences on the north side of 23rd Street is the Fifth Avenue Hotel, facing Madison Square.

West 23rd Street, Looking East toward Sixth Avenue (1975)

23rd Street is now a wide, busy, crosstown artery and almost entirely commercial. In 1936 the motor bus replaced the streetcar. The Sixth Avenue elevated line, with its station at 23rd Street, was demolished in 1939. A branch of the New York subway system was opened on Sixth Avenue to take its place in 1940. All the buildings visible in the 1874 photo have been demolished. The Masonic Temple was torn down in 1910; the present 19-story Masonic Hall Building was erected on the site. The six-story brick apartment on the northwest corner of 23rd Street and Sixth Avenue restored some residential character to this part of 23rd Street in 1959. A variety of commercial buildings have been erected on the north side of 23rd Street since 1885. For many years the street supported stores such as Best's, Stern's, McCreery's and LeBoutillier. A 14-story office building took the place of the Fifth Avenue Hotel in 1908 and Le Brun's Metropolitan Tower rose in 1909. (11/4/75; 1:50.)

East 23rd Street, East from Fifth Avenue to Broadway (1911)

The corner where Fifth Avenue and Broadway meet and where the Flatiron Building stands has always held a reputation for being the windiest corner in town. This photo supports this contention. East 23rd Street was a busy traffic artery and a desirable shopping area, with many converted former dwellings as well as newer commercial buildings. The eight-story Hotel Bartholdi, built in 1885 at the southeast corner of Broadway and East 23rd Street, was named after the sculptor of the Statue of Liberty. It was home for many sportsmen attending events at nearby Madison Square Garden. William Jennings Bryan often visited when campaigning. The American Art Galleries occupied space in the buildings on each side of the hotel until 1922, when they moved uptown and later became part of the Parke-Bernet Galleries. On the left side of 23rd Street is the southern end of Madison Square Park, beyond which stands the original building of the Metropolitan Life Insurance Co.

East 23rd Street, East from Fifth Avenue (1974)

The present southeast corner of Broadway and East 23rd Street is empty. In October 1966 the American Art Galleries Building, along with two smaller adjacent buildings to the rear, were completely destroyed by a disastrous fire which caused the death of 13 firemen. The Bartholdi Building, no longer a hotel, was badly damaged in a fire in 1970 and was torn down. The demolition of the four buildings created a large parking lot. There is little change in either the Flatiron Building corner or in 23rd Street east of the parking lot, where several of the former dwellings and older loft buildings continue to remain useful as business buildings. The Metropolitan Life Insurance Co. has refaced the exterior of its original building. (9/30/74; 12:40.)

East 23rd Street, Looking toward the Beginning of Madison Avenue (1894)

The ten-story white marble structure facing Madison Square is the Metropolitan Life Insurance Co. building, designed by Napoleon Le Brun and Sons and built in 1890-93. Organized in 1866, by 1890 the company had become the leading life insurance company in America. To carry out its impressive plan to erect one of the country's great buildings, the company had to acquire the necessary land as it became available and then build on each plot. By 1909 the building was complete, filling the entire block bounded by 23rd and 24th Streets and by Madison and Fourth Avenues. Adjoining the building stands the Madison Square Presbyterian Church, erected in 1853-54. From 1880 until 1918 its pastor was Dr. Charles H. Parkhurst, the reformer whose efforts helped clear the city government of widespread crime and corruption.

East 23rd Street, Looking toward the Beginning of Madison Avenue (1974)

In 1903 the Metropolitan Life Insurance Co. acquired the southeast corner of Madison Avenue and 24th Street, where Dr. Parkhurst's church stood. Arrangements were made to erect a new church on the northeast corner of 24th Street to take care of the congregation. The new church, a very beautiful building designed by Stanford White, was completed by 1906, whereupon the old brownstone church was torn down. The Metropolitan then completed the last unit in its original plan by building a 700-foot tower on the 24th Street corner. With this construction the Metropolitan Tower became the tallest building in the world from 1909 until 1912, when the Woolworth Building was erected. By 1918 the Metropolitan was able to purchase the new church. After only 12 years of use this outstanding piece of architecture was demolished. The Metropolitan built a 15-story annex in place of it. The insurance firm gradually acquired the entire block from 23rd and 25th Streets and from Madison to Fourth Avenues and constructed a building much larger than the original, in three sections: in 1931-32, 1937-42 and 1948-50. The edge of this building is seen at the extreme left. By 1955 the older building, except for the tower, had been completely "modernized," robbing it of its architectural merit. (12/6/74; 12:35.)

West 42nd Street, Looking West toward Sixth Avenue (1900)

The buildings on the north side of 42nd Street, more than halfway toward Sixth Avenue, are situated in a favored location—facing Bryant Park, which offers light, trees, a view and a pleasant place in which to walk or sit. Originally a potter's field, Bryant Park was for five years the site of the Annual Fair of the American Institute and the famous Crystal Palace, which was destroyed by fire in 1858. The park was later twice torn up for subway construction. The horsecars were run by the 42nd Street, Manhattanville and St. Nicholas Avenue Railway as a crosstown line between the Weehawken Ferries at the west terminal and the Hunters Point Ferry to Long Island City at the east end. On the right is part of the West Presbyterian Church, erected in 1862. The construction of the adjoining Spalding Building in 1890 marked the beginning of the change of this block from residential to business. Several business signs have begun to appear on the former brownstone residences; the sign seen over the near horsecar marks the Conservatory of Music. The large stone building with the one-story mansard roof is the Harmonie Club, a German society. The Sixth Avenue elevated (its 42nd Street station seen at the end of the block) operated for the first time on June 5, 1878 and continued to run for 61 years.

West 42nd Street, Looking West toward Sixth Avenue (1974)

All the buildings up to Sixth Avenue in the 1900 photo are gone, along with the "el," horsecars, gas streetlights and Belgian block paving. Only Bryant Park, on the left, remains. On the right is the 32-story Salmon Tower, built in 1926. Adjoining on the left, and built in 1912 on the site of the West Presbyterian Church, is the former Aeolian Hall (Warren & Wetmore, architects), where George Gershwin introduced his *Rhapsody in Blue* with Paul Whiteman's orchestra in 1924. The building is now the Graduate School and University Center of the City University of New York.

The building with the curved front is the Grace Building, built 1970-72 on the site of Stern Brothers Department Store, which stood here from 1913 to 1969, having previously operated on West 34th Street for 36 years. The building at the northeast corner was built in 1906 as the seven-story Bryant Park Arcade. It was raised an additional eight stories in 1932 to become the present Bryant Park Building. The outline of the top of the former Stern store building can be seen on the east wall of the Bryant Park Building. (12/10/74; 12:35.)

North Side of West 57th Street, Looking West toward Sixth Avenue (1890)

By 1880, 57th Street, a wide thoroughfare without tracks or horsecars and located in the fashionable district uptown, was lined with elegant brownstone residences. Among the well-known New York families who resided there were the Roosevelts, Auchinclosses, Sloanes and Rogers. The signal tower of the Sixth Avenue "el" is visible above 57th Street; the line terminated at 59th Street. The church with the tall spire between Sixth and Seventh Avenues is the Calvary Baptist Church, built in 1883. Beyond the church, at the northwest corner of Seventh Avenue, stands the 11-story Osborn apartment building (Charles C. Haight, architect), a pioneer apartment house and the tallest in the city when it was built in 1885. The spire seen in the distance above the signal tower belongs to the Church of the Strangers, located just beyond Eighth Avenue.

North Side of West 57th Street, Looking West toward Sixth Avenue (1975)

Only two buildings have survived from 1890. The Osborn at the northwest corner of Seventh Avenue is visible at the far left, silhouetted against the taller light mass of the Henry Hudson Hotel. The other building is a four-story brownstone, renovated for business. It is located below the low corner of the "Tow Away Zone" sign, left of center. 57th Street is now characterized by heavy auto traffic and high-rise buildings with smart shops. The "el" has been gone since 1924. In 1929 the Calvary Baptist Church took down its splendid building, reinstalling the church as the central portion of the bottom three stories of the tall Salisbury Hotel building. An imitation church tower on the front of the roof hides the building's water tanks and also carries on the church motif. No. 7 (right), the four-story store and business building with the Georgian brick front, was at one time the brownstone home of the financier and philanthropist Adolph Lewisohn. No. 9, the 50-story building with the curved front, was completed in 1973 (Gordon Bunshaft of Skidmore, Owings & Merrill, architect). It is unusual in design and construction methods, with tinted glass curtain walls and marble edges. The structure is similar in design to the Grace Building, by the same architect, on West 42nd Street. (3/25/75; 11:35.)

East 86th Street, Looking East from Lexington Avenue (1914)

Yorkville was originally a small village along the old Boston Post Road (now Third Avenue), extending from about 80th to 86th Streets and from Park to Third Avenues. In the late eighteenth century a number of German families settled in the village, making it attractive for German immigrants. Yorkville became the principal German community in Manhattan. 100-foot-wide East 86th Street is the heart of the neighborhood, its business and entertainment center. There are several theaters visible, among them the Orpheum, showing a Mary Pickford movie. The large six-story building on the right, behind the middle of the second car of the Third Avenue elevated train, is the popular Yorkville Casino. On the far left, the Y.M.C.A. building is closed for repairs. Transportation for this area was excellent, consisting of a subway line, two elevated railroads and six surface car lines, including the 86th Street crosstown line, which carried passengers across Central Park to the West Side. The two gentlemen in the Model T Ford are evidently waiting for their driver.

East 86th Street, Looking East from Lexington Avenue (1975)

East 86th Street, its sidewalks crowded with shoppers, is still the hub of Yorkville. Gimbels has opened a new 12-story branch on the northwest corner of Lexington Avenue and 86th Street. The Y.M.C.A. building is gone and the only remaining theater from 1914 is Loew's Orpheum, with a less ornate sign. Only the east edge of the third building on the right is visible in the 1914 photo. The other structures up to Third Avenue were demolished to make way for the 35-story Fairmount Manor apartment building erected in 1966 on the southwest corner of Third Avenue. The four-story corner building across Third Avenue remains, minus the cupola of the corner tower. Just beyond, on the site of the Yorkville Casino, is the seven-story Robert F. Wagner office building. It was built in 1966-67 with a movie theater at street level. The 32-story Newbury apartment building on the left was built in 1970. (High-rise apartment buildings, of which five appear in this photo, are beginning to dominate the area—to the consternation of people who feel that "overloading" will destroy Yorkville's neighborhood character.) The bus in the photo takes passengers to the West Side. (12/2/75; 11:50.)

East 94th Street, Looking East from Fifth Avenue (1900)

By 1900 the side streets off upper Fifth Avenue were fairly well built up with expensive four-story and basement homes. The fronts were more ornate than those of the older Italianate brownstones, which were going out of fashion, but the general plan was the same. Fifth Avenue corner lots were quite costly. Those above 90th Street were the last to be built on. The area from about East 88th to East 96th Streets and from Fifth to Lexington Avenues is known as Carnegie Hill;

Andrew Carnegie had built the largest mansion on Fifth Avenue at 91st Street in 1900-02. The heavy dark-brick crenellated towers rising on the left belong to one of the largest armories in the city, built 1888-96 to house the Squadron Troop A (Cavalry) in its Madison Avenue side and the Eighth Regiment (founded in 1847) in its Park Avenue section.

East 94th Street, Looking East from Fifth Avenue (1975)

There has been little change on the north side of East 94th Street except for alterations on the fronts of the second and third residences. The Willard Straight residence, one of the last mansions built on Fifth Avenue and designed in the Federal style by Delano and Aldrich, was erected on the northeast corner in 1914-15. After Straight's death in 1918, it was occupied by Judge Elbert H. Gary and later by Mrs. Harrison Williams. In 1952 the house was renovated for use by the National Audubon Society. Designated a city landmark, it has housed the International Center of Photography since 1974. The south side of East 94th Street has had several residential buildings added since 1900, the most important being the 13-story apartment building built in 1927 on the southeast corner of Fifth Avenue. The former Squadron A Armory, in the center of the photo, which was famous for many years for indoor polo matches, no longer exists. The west wall and towers (on Madison Avenue) were preserved as a city landmark; the rest of the building was demolished, and a new intermediate school was built on the Park Avenue front, with a park and playground behind it. The armory towers and wall serve as a background and protection for the playground. (1/6/75; 11:50.)

East 116th Street, Looking West from Lexington Avenue (1915)

Like 125th Street, 116th Street is an active, wide crosstown thoroughfare from the East River to Morningside Avenue. This section of East Harlem was developed during the 1880s with the familiar New York brownstone residences and walk-up apartments. One block west is the elevated crossing of the New York Central and New Haven Railroads on Park Avenue. The Subway Café, on the right-hand corner, anticipates the opening of the Lexington Avenue subway by three years. On the third floor of the same building, above Dr. Cohen the dentist, is a chemist advertising his laboratory with signs in both English and Italian. The five-story apartment building on the left has a painted sign on the east wall, advertising Bloomingdale's Department Store at Third Avenue and East 60th Street. Transportation gave easy access to the rest of the city.

East 116th Street, Looking West from Lexington Avenue (1975)

Today, East 116th Street is clogged with automobiles, trucks and buses. The second language on various signs is now Spanish instead of Italian. Many of the older buildings remain, but, on the right, four brownstone residences were later replaced by a motion picture theater which in turn became a supermarket. Farther up the block, two six-story apartment houses have been built. A signal tower has been erected over the railroad tracks on the Park Avenue elevated and, on the northwest corner, fried chicken is now sold on the site of the former saloon. The sign for Bloomingdale's on the apartment building on the left is still legible after 60 years. (3/18/75; 11:55.)